S0-BRC-527

PAULINE AND JOHANNINE MYSTICISM

PAULINE AND JOHANNINE MYSTICISM

Sister Sylvia Mary, C.S.M.V.

Darton, Longman & Todd

London

Darton, Longman & Todd Ltd.
64 Chiswick High Road
London W.4

248
Sy58

155597

First published 1964
© Sister Sylvia Mary, C.S.M.V., 1964

Printed in Great Britain by
W. & J. Mackay & Co Ltd, Chatham

Contents

To
SUSAN, my Mother
whose loving interest has been
so great an encouragement

Introduction

IN ALL created life in this world that is below the life of
man, who has dominion over this earth, there is no
instinct that is wasted. Animal life is, in a sense, more
complete than human life: its desires are desires which can
find satisfaction here and now; its instinctive urges are
cause for wonder at the perfection of their creation. Man
alone finds in himself, and has always found, a sense of
incompleteness: the world which he rules, and can mould
to his own purposes if he so wills, yet leaves him with the
conviction—a universal conviction—that this is not for him
the end of all. With the appearance of man on this earth
came also the thought of God, his creator and his end, to be
worshipped and adored. It is this that distinguishes man
from the animal creation: it is his great and fundamental
dignity. As a result of modern research and discoveries
both in the history of religions and in depth-psychology, it
is now being realised that this hunger and thirst for the
things of the spirit and for the divine is as old as mankind
itself. Everywhere, in the most archaic forms of religion,
this thirst for the spiritual shows itself: the mystical urge.

Mysticism is not something to which we can give any
definite meaning. There have been and are many forms of
mysticism in this world. Fundamentally it can probably
best be described as the desire for union with the power
that manifests itself in the world, for the 'wholly other' or
the 'wholly immanent', for that which is above and beyond
all, and yet contains all being in itself and pervades the

universe. It is the longing to find the invisible and the eternal, for, in words familiar to all Christians, 'the things which are seen are temporal; the things which are not seen are eternal'. The many ways and forms in which this desire has manifested itself cannot be dealt with here, since the object of this brief study is that form of mysticism which alone can be called 'Christian mysticism': a form entirely unique in the history of religions, and which, as Christians, we believe to be infinitely superior to every other form of mysticism, for it is the very Truth itself—the Truth which sets us free. It is the 'light of life'. Moreover, it has gathered up into itself, in the course of its history, many streams of perception and devotion.

Christianity is Christ, and all Christian mysticism is fundamentally 'Christ mysticism'. The Synoptic Gospels are full of this Christ mysticism: it is central to them, but it is not expressly dealt with or developed. We have but to think of such sayings as 'The kingdom of heaven is within you', or 'among you' or those parting words of Christ 'Lo, I am with you always, even unto the end of the world', to see how true this is. Again, in the Synoptists alone do we find the accounts of the Transfiguration, with all its tremendous mystical implications. Yet the Messianic secret is kept; the Bridegroom has come, but the mystery is veiled, so that it will be found only by them that seek, and can be disclosed only to those who have eyes to see and ears to hear. It is a 'hidden' mystery, the great 'secret' which has been in the Heart and Mind of God from all eternity, but which can only now be disclosed, after centuries of preparation. The mystery is so great and withal so perfectly simple that even the disciples themselves, those who were closest to the Master in his lifetime, were slow to grasp its meaning. Truly God is a hidden God! His ways are so simple and yet so mysterious that the children to whom he has given such great powers cannot make themselves small enough or simple enough to understand his own simplicity. It has ever been thus, and who can wonder, for he who is so lowly and so simple is the great Lord of all, and contains in himself all the wonders of beauty—riches past our conceiving.

In the Pauline and Johannine writings the mystical implications of the Incarnation are developed, and if we would understand the fundamental meaning of our life 'in Christ' we must turn to these writings, and seek to understand the message they give, remembering that 'the mystical sense of Scripture has always been the cornerstone of orthodoxy'.[1]

[1] J. H. Walgrave, O.P.: *Newman the Theologian*, p. 129.

'Holy Scripture is called the Heart of Christ, because it reveals his Heart.' *St Thomas Aquinas*

I

The Mysticism of the Old Testament

ONE OF the characteristics of our time is that owing to the extremely swift means of communication between widely separated countries there is growing up in this world a much clearer understanding between different peoples—an understanding which later ages may look back upon as one of the greatest achievements of our day. The traditions and outlook of the most diverse cultures are becoming, as it were, common property. Television brings before us Buddhist monks at prayer, as well as the pomps and ceremonies of the Church in Rome. The impression given in this way, though actually to a great extent superficial, nevertheless remains deeply imprinted on our minds, and the predominantly contemplative bent of the great religions of the East has made an immense impression on our more practically-minded West. The result is that the rich contemplative and mystical tradition of our own Christian Church is often ignored or lightly passed over. We consider the great value of Christianity to lie in her high ethical and moral code, her works of charity, the 'agape' which pours itself out in ministering to the sick and needy, for we seldom forget the words of Christ, 'Inasmuch as ye did it to one of these my little ones, ye did it unto me.' In this we are right—it *is* the great and distinctive glory of Christianity, that which places our 'incarnational religion' above every other in this world.   Yet this must not be allowed to blind us to the fact that from the very beginning the true source of all Christian life and work, the foundation upon which they can alone be truly built, is union with Jesus Christ himself.   It is this personal element in Christian mysticism which sets it apart from every other form of mysticism, and which gives it a realism and depth which cannot be found elsewhere.   Behind it lies a long stream of tradition drawn from various sources and forming one rich whole.

However much we may speak of the 'transcendent' God of the Old Testament, the purely mystical element in Hebrew religion is never lacking; in fact, it lies behind it all, and is the basis of all the writings, from the very earliest books of the 'Torah' to so late a book as that of Daniel. The Yahwist writer whose work is predominant in the Book of Genesis infused into his account of the traditions of the patriarchs a deep, pure spirituality.   In his narrative of Abraham and his response to the call of God we have the record of a life of such close communion with God that we are left with a sense of wonder that such intimacies could have been handed down to posterity.   God spoke to this wandering Semite who believed his word, and committed himself unreservedly to the unknown way in perfect trust —a trust that never failed through the most searching tests.

Jacob, going towards Haran, came to a certain place at sunset, and taking some of the stones he found there he put them for his pillow and lay down to sleep.   As he slept he saw a ladder set up upon earth, the top of which reached to heaven, and the angels of God ascended and descended upon it—words which are familiar to us all because of the use made of them by Jesus.

And behold, the Lord stood above it, and said: I am the God of Abraham, thy father, and the God of Isaac: the land whereon thou liest, to thee will I give it and to thy seed; and thy seed shall be as the dust of the earth, and thou shalt spread abroad to the west and to the east, and to the north and to the south; and in thee and in thy seed shall all the families of the earth be blessed: and behold I am with thee in all places whither thou goest . . . I will not leave thee until I have done that which I have spoken to thee of. (Gen. 28: 10ff.)

These words contain the very substance of the hope of the Old Testament: the promise of land and posterity, but also the assurance of God's constant presence and tender care. And Jacob, waking from sleep, said, 'Surely the Lord is in this place, and I knew it not.' And he was afraid and said, 'How dreadful is this place! This is none other but the house of God and this is the gate of heaven.' Here is pure mystical experience, expressed with a simplicity and directness that have seldom been surpassed. St Theresa of Avila, with her penetrating insight into the ways of mystical experience, speaking of the 'mystical betrothal', said that she did not realise at the time what was happening, but afterwards she was *convinced* that she had been in God and God in her—a conviction nothing could ever shake.

Elijah, that great mystical prophet who was seen communing with Jesus on the Mount of Transfiguration, was fleeing from his enemies when he came to Beersheba, where he left his servant and went a day's journey alone into the wilderness. There, coming to a juniper tree, he sat down under it and asked God that he might die: 'It is enough now, Lord; take away my life.' And as he lay there and slept an angel touched him and said 'Arise and eat', and he looked, and there beside him was bread and water, which he ate and drank, and lay down again to sleep. A second time the angel touched him, and said 'Arise and eat; because the journey is too great for thee.' Elijah rose and ate, and in the strength of that food went forty days and forty nights to Horeb, the Mount of God. There, in a cave, he heard the 'still, small voice' of God, and when he heard it he wrapped his face in a mantle and went out, and there the Lord spoke to him. A most lovely account of mystical experience.

In both these cases the experience came from God either directly, or by his angel, by night, to men weary and asleep. The experience is entirely unsought: there are no special attitudes or techniques employed to produce them, as we find almost invariably in other cultures and traditions. There is no auto-suggestion here, but an open-ness to the Divine Presence, the capacity to hear the 'still, small voice' and to feel the presence of God's holiness. 'Be still then, and know that I am God. . . . The God of Jacob is our refuge' (Ps. 46: 10, 11). The psalms, which are the great traditional prayers of the Jewish and Christian churches, are full of aspirations and longings for God:

'Like as the hart desireth the water-brooks, so longeth my soul after thee, O God.' (Ps. 42: 1.) 'My soul thirsteth for God, even for the living God.' (42: 2.) What depths of mystical experience lay behind the familiar words of Psalm 23:

> The Lord is my shepherd, therefore can I lack nothing.
> . . . He leadeth me forth beside the waters of comfort.
> . . . Yea, thou I walk through the valley of the shadow of
> death, I will fear no evil; for thou art with me.

What sublime confidence and spiritual insight are expressed in Psalm 139:

If I climb up into heaven thou art there: if I go down to hell thou art there also. If I take the wings of the morning: and remain in the uttermost parts of the sea: even there shall thy hand lead me: and thy right hand shall hold me. If I say, Peradventure the darkness shall cover me: then shall my night be turned to day. Yea, the darkness is no darkness with thee, but the night is as clear as day: the darkness and light are both alike to thee.

Moses, who was to see God 'face to face' and speak to him as 'a man speaketh to his friend', first saw him in the Burning Bush when he led his father's flock to Horeb, the mount of God. An angel appeared in the midst of the fire, and the bush, despite the flame, was not consumed. By appearing to Moses in the thorn bush God conveyed to him the knowledge that he suffered along with his suffering people Israel. There, too, Moses was taught that nothing existed without the divine presence. The Fathers of the Church saw in the mysterious 'angel of the Lord' who appeared in the fire the Son of God, and interpreted the apparition in the Burning Bush as a manifestation of the Second Person of the Blessed Trinity, revealing himself as the Saviour of his people. God showed that he was not aloof or indifferent, but intervened in earthly affairs. Though Moses was the 'great prophet', he was also a very great mystic. Under his influence the children of Israel were able to perceive the crossing of the Red Sea and the deliverance out of Egypt as a miracle, and it is to this perception that we must attribute the coming into being of 'that which is called Israel in the life of the spirit' (M. Buber)—that tremendous influence in the religious history of mankind. Miracle, from the historical approach, may be regarded as an abiding astonishment. The real meaning of miracle is that in the amazing event the current system of cause and effect becomes, as it were, transparent, and permits a glimpse of that sphere where God's power is at work. To live with 'miracle' is to recognise this power to be at work on every given occasion. Even the most ordinary things, seen in this light, can be 'wonders', however small or trifling, and to live with this sense of wonder at the merciful orderings of God's providence *is*, in a very true sense, to live a life of contemplation. It can become a sure foundation for the life of faith, a personal conviction that nothing can shake. This was the secret of Abraham and Moses, and of all the great figures of the Old Testament. In the accounts of the crossing of the Red Sea and again in that of the passage of Jordan under Joshua, we must think not so much of the outward sign as of the hidden message of faith. The Cross and Resurrection of Christ have for us the same meaning as the 'wonder' of the Exodus had for the Israelites: the veil of earthbound knowledge was broken through, and the hidden sovereignty of God over nature was seen in the raising of the First-begotten from the dead.

In the great event on Sinai, God called Moses from the Mount:

> This shalt thou say to the children of Israel: Ye have seen how I bare you on eagles' wings, and brought you to myself . . . if ye obey my voice and keep my covenant then ye shall be a peculiar treasure to me above all people.

On the third day God suddenly descended and manifested himself in the midst of the radiant fire to encounter his chosen ones. The whole of Sinai smoked, and the voice of God himself issued from the fire. Those who were called to the Mount were filled with marvelling wonder, and out of this primitive tradition grew Israel's lasting sense of the danger and sublimity involved in living so close to God, and their experienced need of 'covering' of 'shield' against the wrath of God. Such covering was felt to fit men for intercourse with God. In a very real sense 'atonement' is fundamentally a sheltering, a covering, though in a more profound form. The command of Jesus 'Abide in me' thus answers to one of the most deeply felt needs of men's hearts. The flame that Moses had seen in the bush was now seen on the Mount by all Israel, but the top of the mountain was covered by a cloud, and into this cloud Moses alone entered, remaining there forty days and forty nights.

One of the commands given to Moses during this first sojourn on the Mount is of special importance:

> Speak thou also unto the children of Israel, saying, Verily my sabbaths shall ye keep: for it is a sign between me and you throughout your generations; that ye may know that I am the Lord that doth sanctify you. (Ex. 31: 13.) The children of Israel shall keep the sabbath, to observe the sabbath throughout their generations for a perpetual covenant. (v. 16.)

In Israel alone the sabbath is 'holy unto the Lord', and there alone is it brought into connection with the creation. This doctrine of the connection of the sabbath with the creation is inseparable from Moses. If the sabbath articulates 'universal time', then it cannot enter in at a certain moment, since it is always there, but it can be discovered and revealed at a certain moment, and for this no less a person than Moses was needed. In post-exilic times the sabbath laws became a burden to the Jewish people, but when the sabbath first appeared the whole emphasis was on 'rest': 'It shall be a sabbath of rest unto you.' When Jesus claimed the sabbath for his own he gave it the early, original meaning: 'The Son of Man is lord also of the sabbath'; 'Come unto me . . . and I will give you rest.' 'There remaineth yet a rest for the people of God', says the writer of Hebrews, and here, in Hebrews 4: 9, the word κατάπαυσις of the previous verse drops into the word 'σαββατισμός' speaking of the rest of the world to come. When, in the Last Discourses in the Fourth Gospel Jesus says 'My peace I give unto you' it is that eternal peace which is at the very Heart of God, but which the human race is so slow to understand and accept.

When Moses came down from his second sojourn on the Mount his face shone so that the people could not look upon him unless there was a veil over his face—a veil which for the Jews was not taken away in the reading of the Old Testament, but which was 'done away in Christ' (2 Cor. 3: 14). Moses was transformed by the revelation of God and his communing with him, and thus became the embodiment of God's glory for Israel, foreshadowing the revelation of the Lord on the Mount of Transfiguration. In the encounter of Moses with God the eternal broke through and manifested itself in the temporal as never again till the Incarnation of the Son of God himself, the 'Light that lighteth every man', for 'Yahweh spoke to Moses face to face as a man is wont to speak to his friend'.

*   *   *

The writings of the eighth-century prophets are some of the greatest and most beautiful in the world. Isaiah, another great mystic, was in the Temple when he received the great vision described in the sixth chapter. Though what he here describes is definite fact, and these were the spiritual processes he passed through at the beginning of his ministry, it is written by one who had felt the prophetic office to be the burden of a lifetime. He sees the whole world lying in sin, but nevertheless filled with the glory of God. The note struck in this vision of his call is the keynote of his entire prophecy. 'The Holy One of Israel' becomes in Isaiah the expression of deity, prevailing over all others by its potency, and his great Trisagion has rung down through the ages. He received this vision in the year 'King Uzziah died'. Probably, being of noble birth and connected with the court, the dramatic life of this king made a great impression upon him, for Uzziah, after fifty years of glorious reign, was struck down with leprosy, and ended his life in a lazar house. It was at this strange, bewildering time that Isaiah received his call. Though this vision took place in the Temple, there is, strangely enough, no mention of sacrifices. The vision was of a Personal Presence behind all the outward forms of religion, and in the shuddering sense of the Divine Presence and God's sovereignty he recoiled from the low religious views of his time. 'Mine eyes have seen the King, the Lord of Hosts' (Is. 6: 9). Nothing will probe the shell of callousness that surrounds our souls but the touching of the Divine and human spirits. He heard the cherubim crying to one another, 'Holy, holy, holy, is the Lord of Hosts: the whole earth is full of his glory.' Here holiness received a new depth of meaning. Originally 'holiness' has no moral connotation—none of the attributes of God are synonymous with 'holiness', they are rather elements in it. 'The holy one', simply, is God. 'Kadosh' ('holy') was not primarily an epithet for God—it expressed the idea of God.

The thought of God's holiness is distinctive of all the Isaianic writings, and the result was a new conception of sin: not simply the breaking of ritual enactments, but a sense of 'profaneness' in the presence of the All-Holy One.

'The house', says Isaiah, 'was filled with smoke.' The smoke, surely, that arises where holiness and sin touch each other. What the prophet felt must have been

> the dim-eyed shame, the distraction, the embarrassment, the blinding shock of a personal encounter . . . a Personal Presence which apprehended and overwhelmed him (G. Adam Smith: *Isaiah*, p. 68).

'Holiness' is a very mysterious conception, whose origins are hidden in the mists of antiquity. A recent writer, discussing this concept, comes to the conclusion that it is most perfectly expressed by the idea of 'perfect vision'. By this he means, as far as I can understand it, that from all eternity God has seen and known ALL. Every discovery and every vision that can come to man has always been there in God, and man slowly, by glimpses here and there, discovers bit by bit what God has always seen and known. When we add to this the knowledge that 'God is love' we begin to realise how mysterious and incomprehensible is the God of Holiness whom we worship. If we believe that God created everything *ex nihilo*, out of nothing, then there is nothing that is not utterly dependent on the 'perfect vision' of God, the Creator and Sustainer of all. (See O. R. Jones: *The Concept of Holiness*, 1951.)

This idea of the 'holy' only received its full expression in the Incarnation. In Christ, who is the 'light of the world', we can begin to see what lay behind that otherwise almost inexplicable conception—a conception not limited to the Old Testament, though it is there that it finds its

highest conception in the ancient world. In the New
Testament God becomes not less, but more holy—the
distance between his holiness and our sinfulness is increased
and not diminished: it is made absolute. For Isaiah the
great tragedy is that the people did not *know* God: 'Israel
doth not know: my people doth not consider.' They
believed in the almighty Yahweh, but they did not know
his nature. He said to the people:

> This is the rest wherewith ye may cause the weary to rest;
> and this is the refreshing; yet they would not hear. But
> the word of the Lord was to them precept upon precept
> (Is. 28: 12).

The message Isaiah sought to convey to his people was one
of confidence and trust in God, but they would not hear:

> For thus saith the Lord God, the Holy One of Israel, In
> returning and rest shall ye be saved; in quietness and in
> confidence shall be your strength: and ye would not (30:
> 15).

Though the Lord may give them the bread of adversity and
of affliction, yet 'thine ear shall hear a word behind thee,
saying, This is the way, walk ye in it, when ye turn to the
right hand, and when ye turn to the left' (30: 21).

This is the pure mysticism of the Old Testament—a life
lived in God, in obedience to the divine voice and confidence in the divine providence. It is open to all to live
in this way, though only to the great prophets and mystics—
who are, as it were, the eyes of the people—are mystical
experiences given, with all they entail of responsibility and
suffering, since the prophets are the bearers of the divine
message which was the very life of Israel. Jeremiah, who
knew so much of this burden and suffering, is the prophet
of the inner life of union with God. During the Exile,

when all those things which distract men and turn their eyes to outward things were torn from them, some of the Israelites were able to find God speaking in their hearts, and their whole outlook was interiorised. Jeremiah's record of familiar intercourse with God is of great value, throwing a new light on the way of God and the way of man. In the light of his inner union with God he looked about him and saw the true meaning of sin, its essential roots. He realised, with the vividness that comes only to the mystic, the wonder of God's love, of his yearning longing for the response of love from his people. Israel's forgetfulness of that love seemed to him to be the very essence of sin, and this recognition of the *inwardness* of sin, as apart from failure in ritual observance, is the great contribution made by Jeremiah to the truth about man. He saw that sin begins in stubbornness of heart, and therefore condemned as futile the outward worship in which the heart did not take part.

They have forsaken thee, the fountain of living waters (17:13).

Because of his covenant-love God cannot punish without suffering to himself: Jeremiah shows us the cross at the very heart of God. In a very striking passage he summarises the whole history of the Israelites:

Thou hast brought forth thy people Israel out of the land of Egypt with signs and with wonders, and with a strong hand, and with a stretched out arm, and with great terror; and thou hast given them this land, which thou didst swear to their fathers to give them, a land flowing with milk and honey; and they came in and possessed it; but they obeyed not thy voice, neither walked in thy laws; they have done nothing of all that thou commandedst them: therefore thou hast caused all this evil to come upon them (Jer. 32:21ff.).

He had known the love of God:

> The Lord hath appeared of old unto me, saying: Yea, I have
> loved thee with an everlasting love; therefore with loving-
> kindness have I drawn thee (31: 3).

and he is convinced that God will accomplish his redemptive purpose.   He will not again give an external law which
would only be disobeyed, but he will work an inner change
in the heart of man.   How this will be accomplished
Jeremiah cannot tell, though he emphasises the fact that
this 'inner' change is coming, this 'touch' of God in the
heart of man, but does not show how it will be accomplished.   How was the new covenant to be mediated?
Here his vision failed, though he was sure that it would
come:

> This shall be the covenant that I will make with the house of
> Israel: After those days, saith the LORD, I will put my law
> in their inward parts, and write it in their hearts; and will
> be their God, and they shall be my people (31: 33).

He sees a time coming when men shall no longer teach
one another saying, 'Know the Lord: for they shall all
know me, from the least of them unto the greatest of them,
saith the Lord' (31: 34).   In the New Testament there
are between forty and fifty quotations from Jeremiah.

Here, very briefly, we have sketched something of the
mystical and interior life which is characteristic of the Old
Testament, and which formed the background both of St
John and of St Paul, enabling them to interpret the life and
words of Christ and to see their true import.

Centuries later, in the Book of Daniel, we find a striking
account of mystical vision in these apocalyptic writings

which probably greatly influenced the thought of the Jews in the time of Christ.

> And I, Daniel, alone saw the vision, for the men who were with me did not see the vision, but a great trembling fell upon them, and they fled to hide themselves.   Therefore I was left alone and saw this great vision, and there remained no strength in me . . . and behold, a hand touched me . . . and said unto me . . . Fear not!

What a dramatic account of an utterly unexpected vision. It ends up with a beautiful assurance: 'O man greatly beloved, fear not, peace be with you; be strong and of good courage.'   And when he had spoken Daniel was strengthened and able to bear the words addressed to him.

2

'In Christ Jesus'

GOD'S OMNIPRESENCE is, in a sense, the fundamental thought in all mysticism. Mystical experience itself is universal, for all men are made in God's image, and have a capacity for union with God—a capacity which is man's distinctive prerogative. St Teresa was given to understand in her prayer that there are secrets of God's omnipresence which it did not appertain to her to penetrate, but declared, 'All I know is that I tell the truth; and that I shall never believe that any soul who does not possess this certainty has ever been really united to God' (Interior Castle, 5th Mansion). She was shown that there are different modes of God's Being in creation, and, though he is omnipresent, only *persons* are capable of receiving the inflowing of the divine personal life, for God's Being is *personal* being, and only those who have real spiritual capacity can be the recipients of the divine grace. Man alone is capable of responding to this supernatural grace of God, and that sets him above all other created beings.

Few words through the ages have been given more varied interpretations than 'mysticism', and this is scarcely surprising, for it is, in itself, always something mysterious. Probably for most people it implies some experience of things outside the known and visible world of sense and sense-perception—some awareness of the 'wholly-other',

which, from the very earliest appearance of man on this
earth, has apparently made itself felt. There is in man a
natural thirst and longing for union with God, with the
power that rules in this world. Recent studies have
shown this to be apparent even in the most backward and
primitive cultures. In the Mediterranean world into which
St Paul was called to carry the Gospel of Christ there was a
very widespread desire for mystical union with the divine.
It is said that in Egypt many priests spent their whole lives
in contemplation, and the Greek 'mystery-religions' be-
trayed the same mystical *attrait*, which expressed itself in
sacramental forms. Thus, quite apart from Judaism, there
was a very real preparation for the Incarnation amongst
other peoples of the world.

This 'natural' mysticism is common to all men, but the
Christian revelation has brought something new into this
world. God, who is not only transcendent but also inter-
venes in the affairs of this world, has 'in Christ' revealed
himself to us as far as that is possible—that is, in the way in
which we can glimpse something of the true mystery of the
divine life, of the life of the Blessed Trinity, which is
inaccessible to any created intelligence, and must always
remain for us ineffable and incomprehensible. Though in
course of time the Catholic Church was able to take up
into itself many of the best elements in the mysticism of
the ancient pagan world, thus showing its true catholicity,
we must always keep in mind the essential elements in its
own distinctive mystical and spiritual teaching. Here we
are faced with the mystery of the divine choice, of God's
Love given to those he calls to himself, which illumines
and transforms them. God gives this supernatural life to
those he chooses, and that brings an element of mystery

into the very heart of humanity, for, says St John, 'They are born not of blood, nor of the will of the flesh, nor of the will of man, but of God' (St John 1 : 13). Christians are called to share in divinity, in the supreme mystery of the Eternal, of him who created all things and who keeps them in being. Yet, unlike the ancient 'mysteries', this tremendous mystery is open to all; it is the revelation of the hidden purpose of God, but it is to be proclaimed from the housetops—everything is open in this appeal of divine love. Only those who exclude themselves are excluded: 'Him that cometh to me I will in no wise cast out.' Here is something far more mysterious than any 'nature-mysticism'; here God calls man, created in his image, to share in his own personal life of love, and man is left free to accept or to reject that which is beyond his conceiving.

'In Christ' we are brought into union not with the 'unknown God', but with our 'Heavenly Father', who has in these last days revealed himself to us by his Son, in whom we have received the adoption, and in union with whom we can cry 'Abba, Father'. This union with God in Christ begins here, in this life, but it will only come to its full fruition in heaven, where we shall be like him, for we shall see him as he is: we shall be conformed to the likeness of Christ. The foundation of our 'new life' is union with Christ, and this is far more than a mere restoration of that life which Adam lived in paradise before the Fall, in the childhood of our race. St Paul saw this with immense clarity, and therefore the fundamental expression of his mystical theology was the phrase 'In Christ Jesus'.

The frequency of this expression in his writings is somewhat obscured in translations of the New Testament by the use of such words as 'by Christ' or 'through Christ', which are thought to convey the more exact meaning, but in the original Greek the constant use of 'ἐν χριστῷ Ἰησοῦ' is very striking. This concept of life 'in Christ' seems entirely to have dominated St Paul's thought. Therefore, if we wish to understand something of his conception of our life as Christians, we must try to penetrate behind the surface of his writings and grasp what lay hidden behind this familiar phrase. One of the most important theological discussions of the past century has been concerned with the actual meaning of these words, and since it concerns the nature of our union with Christ it is a question of vital importance. Here we will consider quite briefly some of the suggestions and theories that have been advanced, especially since the impetus given to the discussion by a monograph—'Die Neutestamentliche Formel ''in Christo Jesu'' '—published by A. Deissmann in 1893. Among the various questions that have been raised the first and most important is whether or not St Paul actually used this phrase mystically. Closely connected with this is the further question of the relationship between St Paul's 'en Christo Jesu' and the mystical teaching of St John. Another important point is whether we enter into the life 'in Christ' by faith, or by baptism only. In considering these questions we will seek to draw some light on the mystical teaching both of St Paul and St John.

The constant use of the phrase 'in Christ Jesus' in the Pauline Epistles makes it perfectly clear that this thought of being 'in Christ' dominated his whole outlook. It crops up everywhere, in many varying contexts, and it is therefore not surprising that this phrase should have given rise to much questioning and discussion. In dealing with the various points that have been raised we must, nevertheless, bear in mind the fact that the real background of St Paul's teaching is mystical experience in the truest and deepest sense. Real vision is concrete and brings the knowledge of absolute reality—that reality which man in his inmost being desires above all else. It is also effective: it works the works of God in the divine power. There is in its recipients some of that dynamic force which lies at the very heart of all life and being. In the history of mankind few have shown this more clearly than such great visionaries and mystics as Moses and St Paul. Often, it is true, the phrase 'en Christo' taken simply in its context can have no real mystical connotation, yet when it is placed against the background of the whole Pauline teaching and outlook the mystical sense must be read into it.

Some theologians, however, feel that they cannot describe St Paul's use of 'en Christo' as in any sense mystical. Since St Paul derives everything from the Death and Resurrection of Christ, they insist that there can be nothing 'mystical' in the phrase, but that it denotes, rather, the vital, intimate union of St Paul with Jesus Christ—a union in which we all share (P. Feine). This is perfectly true, but is it not also the heart of all Christian mysticism—indeed, the heart of Christianity itself? Dr Moberly once pointed out that had all Christians been true to their calling we should never have heard of such a thing as 'Christian mysticism', because all Christians would have been mystics (*Atonement and Personality*, p. 316). Again, P. Feine says:

> I cannot regard as mystical a relationship between two persons where each retains his separate individuality (*Apostel Paulus*, p. 568).

This raises two important points. In the first place, he is perfectly right in asserting that in our union with Christ

we do not lose our individuality. It is not correct to say
that for St Paul 'to be in Christ' is to be absorbed in the
heavenly Lord, and that in this union the personality loses
its individuality. Paul remains himself, the life animating
him is lived by him. The believer never ceases to be
himself. Even that familiar verse which at once comes to
our minds in this connection, Galatians 2: 20, where a
fusion of persons might at first sight seem to be suggested,
when considered more carefully does not imply absorption.

> Through the law I died to law—to live for God. I have
> been crucified with Christ: the life I now live is not my life,
> but the life which Christ lives in me; and my present bodily
> life is lived by faith in the Son of God, who loved me and
> sacrificed himself for me.

This is often regarded as the classical instance of St Paul's
mystical thought. Yet, though he here speaks of such
close union with Christ in his crucifixion, and coins a word
to express it '$\sigma\upsilon\nu\epsilon\sigma\tau\alpha\acute{\upsilon}\rho\omega\mu\alpha\iota$', 'con-crucified', this is at once
followed by the words 'the life *I* now live'. He has just
said, 'I have died to the law—to live for God': here God
mysticism and Christ mysticism are closely brought together, and it is followed by the words 'I will not nullify the
grace of God'. In this present life he lives by faith, only
hereafter will he live by sight. 'Christ loved me and
sacrificed himself for me': there is no loss of personality
here: the relationship between Christ and Paul is rather
that of the Old Testament 'I and Thou' than of 'absorption
mysticism'. Again, when St Paul speaks of the future
glory he says 'with Christ' instead of 'in Christ', which,
though it may actually appear less intimate, does serve to
show that neither here nor hereafter is there any 'absorption' in true Christian mysticism. We may illustrate this,

too, by a quotation from Père Teilhard de Chardin:

> Union differentiates. In every organised whole the parts
> perfect themselves and fulfil themselves . . . to accent the
> depth and incommunicability of their egos. The more
> other they become in conjunction, the more they find
> themselves as 'self'. How could it be otherwise, since
> they are steeped in 'Omega'? (*The Phenomenon of Man*,
> p. 262).

Though our union with Christ is a union of person with
Person, in which each retains his individuality, yet one
Person in this partnership is also God: he is divine—'Jesus
Christ, the same yesterday, today and for ever' (Heb. 13:8).
Moreover, it is because of his divinity that it is possible
for us to have this intimate communion with him. The
doctrine of the possibility of this union with Jesus Christ
was slowly developed during the first five centuries of the
Christian era, concluding, as they did, with the great
Christological controversies of the fourth and fifth centuries.
Since Jesus Christ is God, our relationship with him must
of necessity be mystical, mysterious—far more deeply
mysterious than any pure 'God mysticism'—incomprehensible, and entirely *sui generis*.

For St Paul, Christ was not a great historical figure, not
so much a Person of the past as a reality and a power of the
present. His religion is not primarily a doctrine about
Christ, it is fellowship with him, with the

> living and present spiritual Christ who is about him on all
> sides, dwells in him, speaks in and through him (A.
> Deissmann: *St Paul*, p. 124).

In many places, it is true, he uses 'in Christ' simply to refer
to Church membership, as at the end of his Epistles. In
certain other contexts, too, the words cannot have a

'mystical' meaning, as, for example, where he says 'God was in Christ reconciling the world to himself'. Here 'in Christ' is the sphere, the place, in which God worked our redemption. Deissmann thought that St Paul regarded Christ as a kind of spiritual space in which the believer lives, as in an atmosphere, and maintained that 'en Christo' had this mystical meaning every time it was mentioned. Though this cannot really be maintained, in the overwhelming number of cases it must mean what it says; it must be given a 'locative' sense. To be 'in Christ' is to possess an entirely different kind of life:

> Therefore, if any man be in Christ, he is an entirely new creature.

He is no longer 'under the Law', but is brought into the freedom of life 'in Christ'. He is 'dead unto sin' and 'alive unto righteousness'. In a sense, then, even when St Paul uses the words merely to refer to Church membership he must have had in his mind his doctrine that every Christian enters into a mysterious union of life and being with Christ.

St Paul appears to use 'in Christ' and 'Christ in us' almost interchangeably, scarcely seeming to notice the difference, and it has been suggested that his thinking was entirely archaic and animistic: that for him Christ works and wells up in us as a Person—not as an impersonal force.[1] The indwelling of the Spirit in the prophets of Israel supplies an analogy, or, for the ancients, the indwelling of demons. Yet here we must insist that Christ's invasion of us takes nothing away but an imperfection. It is an

[1] J. Weiss: 'The form of the idea is entirely archaic, animistic, primitive: it is a second spiritual Being which dwells in Christians.' (ZntW. xix, 1920, p. 131.)

imperfection for a human being to be closed in upon itself. The Divine Persons are entirely opened up to one another, but 'Man has closed up within himself the springs of divine grace' (Philaret of Moscow). At the Fall man obstructed in himself the faculty for communion with God by turning deliberately away from him, but God's plan was not destroyed by man's sin: the vocation of the first Adam was fulfilled in Christ. Now, under the new Covenant, the Holy Spirit opens up man's being to the Person of Christ, and thus raises him to union with God.

Though St Paul's all-absorbing thought was of union with Christ, and he seldom speaks directly of union with God, yet this is definitely implied in such passages as 'From first to last this has been the work of God' (2 Cor. 5: 18), and again: 'God was in Christ reconciling the world to himself' (v. 19). Nor can we for a moment imagine that he, a Jew of the very strictest sect of his religion, could possibly have given his whole-hearted devotion to Jesus his Lord unless he had believed him to be divine. It was through Christ that God redeemed us, and through him that salvation is made available to men; in him we become 'sons of God'. Nevertheless, there is in our union with him no fusion of persons. St Paul never says 'I am Christ'—the Risen and Triumphant Lord is a distinct Person from the Christian who is united with him. So in Galatians 3: 17 St Paul says, 'Ye are all one *in* Christ', but he does not say, 'Ye *are* Christ.' It is important to remember this distinction.

Dr A. Schweitzer, in a book written during a year's furlough in Europe in 1930, has some illuminating passages on St Paul's mysticism, showing that 'God mysticism', if by this we mean becoming one with the 'infinite creative will of God', cannot be realised, and that every attempt to

P.J.M.—C

build a living religion on pure God mysticism has been doomed to failure—it remains a dead thing, whether undertaken by Stoics or by Indian or Chinese thought. They know the direction, but cannot find the way. Man, being finite, cannot comprehend the Infinite and Eternal; the Everlasting God must remain for us men incomprehensible; his ways, as St Paul saw, are 'past finding out'. In Christ Jesus, God's love has been made manifest to us, in him we see God in the only way that we can understand. Through union with him union with God is realised in the only way possible for us. St Paul, by confining himself to seeing sonship to God, realised in union with Christ, was a guiding light, throwing a beam of light on the Eternal, 'based upon the firm foundation of the historical manifestation of Jesus Christ' (*The Mysticism of Paul the Apostle*, p. 379, 3rd ed.).

Dr Schweitzer's chief contribution to the consideration of 'en Christo' and its essential meaning lies in his insistence on its eschatological character. He pointed out the immense importance of eschatology in the thought of St Paul, and spoke of his mysticism as 'eschatological mysticism'. This, he declared, distinguished it from every other form of mysticism, because it related it to the events which are to mark the times of the End. In Daniel's idea of the 'community of saints' he sees the origin of the Catholic conception of the Church.

I saw in the night visions, and behold, with the clouds of heaven there came one like a son of man, and he came to the Ancient of Days and was presented before him. And to him was given dominion and glory and a kingdom, that all peoples nations and languages should serve him; and his dominion is an everlasting dominion, which shall not pass away, and his kingdom one that shall not be destroyed (Dan. 7: 13, 14).

The saints of the Most High shall take the kingdom, and possess the kingdom for ever and ever (7: 22).

In the Similitudes of Enoch, too, we hear of the 'congregation of the righteous' who appear with the Elect, the Holy One, the 'Son of Man'. The idea of the 'community of saints' would thus have been perfectly familiar both to Jesus and to Paul, though in Jewish eschatological thought it was entirely a matter of the future. When the Messiah appeared as a man among men before the beginning of the Kingdom the case was entirely altered, and the idea gained immensely in vitality. The relationship of the Elect with the Messiah came into force here and now, and the Messianic world and the natural world were brought together. St Paul's eschatology led him to maintain that the powers of resurrection manifested in Jesus are, from the moment of his death and resurrection, at work upon those who are the 'elect to the Messianic Kingdom', that is, the members of the Church of Christ. He bases this idea on the relationship of the Elect to Christ in his Kingdom, a view which was the natural outcome of the 'Son of Man' and 'Community of Saints' ideas of Daniel and Enoch. Schweitzer thought that this gave rise to St Paul's 'Christ mysticism', and union with Christ thus becomes the *foundation* upon which the eternal kingdom of heaven rests:

For us there is one God, the Father, from whom all being comes, towards whom we move; and there is one Lord Jesus Christ, through whom all things came to be, and we through him (1 Cor. 8: 6).

As in Adam all men die, so in Christ will all be brought to life; but each in his own proper place: Christ the firstfruits,

and afterwards, at his coming, those who belong to Christ.
Then comes the end, when he delivers up the kingdom to
God the Father (1 Cor. 15: 23).

Our life 'is hid with Christ in God' (Col. 3: 3).

Now this idea, this 'Christ mysticism' did not originate
with St Paul, but with Jesus himself, who brought to an
end that line of development which began with Daniel,
though we must not limit his conception to that set forth
in the Jewish apocalyptic writings.   It is being realised
more and more that Jesus gathered up and fulfilled in himself concepts which are found not only in the Old Testament,
but also in various other cultures of the ancient world concerning the 'Son of Man' or the Man.   In the Prophets the
final tribulation proceeds from God, in Daniel it comes
from the God-opposing powers:

> He shall speak great words against the most High, and shall
> wear out the saints of the most High (Dan. 7: 25).

When persecution becomes very intense, then the Elect
are under the protection of Michael.   This view was
carried to its logical conclusion by Jesus when he insisted
that in the Great Tribulation his followers are in the hand
of God, and that, whether they live or die, they are assured
of participation in the Kingdom.   From this arose the idea
of martyrdom, and its immense influence on the thought
of the early centuries of Christianity.   It is an open question how far Jesus himself was influenced by the concept
of Daniel and Enoch, yet in using this concept he would
have been understood by the Jews of his day.   His own
preaching contained the 'Christ mysticism' which St Paul
was to develop so strongly.   He declared that in fellowship with him his followers had the guarantee of fellowship
in the future with the Son of Man.   He offered this as a

'mystery', and his hearers did not realise that it referred to himself.   This did not really matter, for the vital thing was that they should enter into fellowship with him, not that they should understand how it came about or what all its implications actually were.   Thus in the synoptic Gospels we hear him say, 'Come unto me', 'Learn of me', 'Follow after me'.   Ultimately, everything depends on realised fellowship with Jesus himself.   The one thing needful is not to be offended in him, not to find him a 'stumbling-block': 'Happy is the man that does not find in me a stumbling-block' (Matt. 11: 6).

In the Gospels Jesus gathers his disciples round him that they may be with him, and that they may be made fit, by thus living with the Son of God 'in the flesh', to dwell with God in his eternal Kingdom.   So in his Church, by living contact with Jesus in sacrament and prayer, by hearing the Gospel message, the members of his Body here in this world, in time, may be purged, transformed, and conformed to the image of Christ, the Word made Flesh. Jeremiah and Ezekiel had seen that this was one day to come to pass, but how they could not tell.   Jesus, in his own Person, summed up the whole meaning of the Kingdom of God.   Origen, one of the great Alexandrian Platonists, commenting on St Matthew 18: 23 said:

If ye seek the meaning of 'Theirs is the Kingdom of Heaven', you can say that 'Christ is theirs, since He-is-the-Kingdom'.

John the Baptist had heralded this kingdom—Jesus is the Kingdom which it has pleased God to give to men.   This Kingdom, however, is envisaged as having two stages, an earthly and a heavenly, a present and a future; it is both this-worldly and other-worldly.   Though Jesus is in this world as its King, he dies to enter his heavenly Kingdom. Thus, in the feeding of the multitudes the fundamental significance was not to satisfy their hunger, but that, eating the consecrated food from his hands they should have table-fellowship with him, though they did not realise what that meant.   Though Jesus does not reveal to his hearers the contents of his own self-consciousness, he brings them again and again face to face with the thought that in fellow-ship with him they actually have fellowship with the 'Son of Man'.   In this way he himself taught Christ mysticism in a way his followers might understand, and which was appropriate to the time when he was still walking this earth.

Jesus made an end of the natural world and brought in the Messianic Kingdom in which all Christians share: this was the conviction of the primitive Church.   The Kingdom could not come without the pre-Messianic tribulation, but in his Passion and Death Jesus suffered that tribulation *in himself*, thereby triumphing utterly over all the powers of evil, and bringing in the Kingdom of God:

> Give thanks to the Father who has made you fit to share the heritage of God's people in the realm of light.   He rescued us from the domain of darkness and brought us away into the kingdom of his dear Son, in whom our release is secured and our sins forgiven.   He is the image of the invisible God; his is the primacy over all things . . . he exists before everything, and all things are held together in him. . . . Through him God chose to reconcile the whole universe to himself, making peace through the shedding of his blood upon the cross—to reconcile all things, whether on earth or in heaven, through him alone (Col. 1: 12–17; 20).

3

'Caught up into Paradise'

FROM WHAT did St Paul's 'Christ mysticism' really spring? What was the vital seed that was to shoot up and grow into so mighty a tree, which was to spread its branches into the whole world and have such lasting effects?

There can be little doubt that its origin was in the great vision on the Damascus Road, which is dramatically described in the ninth chapter of the Acts of the Apostles, and again in St Paul's speech before Agrippa which is recorded in Acts 26:

> 'In all the synagogues I tried by repeated punishment to make them renounce their faith; indeed my fury rose to such a pitch that I extended my persecution to foreign cities. On one such occasion I was travelling to Damascus with authority and commission from the chief priests; and as I was on my way, Your Majesty, in the middle of the day I saw a light from the sky, more brilliant than the sun, shining all around me and my travelling-companions. We all fell to the ground, and then I heard a voice saying to me in the Jewish language, "Saul, Saul, why do you persecute me? It is hard for you, this kicking against the goad." I said, "Tell me, Lord, who you are"; and the Lord replied, "I am Jesus, whom you are persecuting. But now, rise to your feet and stand upright. I have appeared to you for a purpose: to appoint you my servant and witness, to testify both to what you have seen and to what you shall yet see of me"' (Acts 26: 11–16).

In Galatians, St Paul mentions the event—his own personal account—briefly and poignantly:

> God, who had set me apart from birth and called me through his grace, chose to reveal his Son to me and through me in order that I might proclaim him among the Gentiles (Gal. 1: 15, 16).

Again, in Ephesians, he says:

> It was by revelation that his secret was made known to me (3: 3).

Clearly, then, for St Paul this vision was the starting-point, *the* great event of his life. There is a touching illustration of this which can only be seen in the Greek New Testament. Each time this vision is described the old Aramaic form of the Apostle's name is used: 'Saoul, Saoul . . .' Those tender accents which fell upon his inward ear as the blinding light flashed upon him could never be forgotten: they were deeply imprinted on his memory—ineffaceable. Christian mystics have noticed that this actually happens when the Lord speaks to them: there is some slight, familiar peculiarity which characterises it and remains imprinted on their hearts.

Though all scholars agree in seeing the importance of this vision in the life of St Paul, all do not give it equal value. Professor Mersch sees in this dramatic encounter 'the seed of all Paulinism'.[1] Dr Schweitzer, however, declares that we really know little of what happened there, and think that St Paul's mystical doctrine of 'being-in-Christ' had no subjective origin, but was merely 'a logical inference from the Christian faith'.[2] Extraordinarily in-

[1] E. Mersch: *The Whole Christ*, p. 84.
[2] op. cit., p. 174.

teresting as his book on St Paul's mysticism is, with its fresh vivid approach, poured out of a heart which is surely close to that of St Paul himself in its utter devotion and passionate zeal, it is not always possible to agree with Dr Schweitzer's conclusions. Here he appears to be strangely contradictory, as, in fact, St Paul sometimes was. He declares that St Paul insists that the truth about Christ is not received from tradition but from revelations of the Spirit of Jesus Christ—a principle he cannot surrender.[1] Yet elsewhere he says that 'the distinctive characteristic of the Pauline doctrine is that it arose out of profound thought' and at the same time out of 'direct experience'. This is true, but surely it is not true that, as he goes on to say, 'the profound thought is primary, because it carries with it an impulse to realisation in experience' (p. 386). This statement seems to place the whole initiative on man's side, and is surely a distortion of the teaching of him whose supreme joy it was that he had been 'apprehended of Christ' in that dramatic encounter which changed his life, since he had not been 'disobedient to the heavenly vision'. We cannot limit what is revealed by God in the rare transforming visions he gives to those who are especially called to reveal his purpose to the world. We must regard the vision before Damascus as one of the great, dynamic experiences given by God to man. Nevertheless, though this vision was the 'starting-point', it must not be isolated.

---

[1] 'Paul, apart from unavoidable concessions to the tradition, abides by the principle that the truth about Christ is not received from traditional narratives and doctrines, but from revelations given by the Spirit of Jesus Christ. This principle he cannot surrender, because his own interpretation of the death and resurrection of Jesus goes far beyond the doctrine applied to him by the tradition, while his view of liberation from the Law is in contradiction to it.' (op. cit., p. 174.)

In his speech before the Jewish mob in Acts 22: 17 St Paul says:

> 'After my return to Jerusalem, I was praying in the Temple when I fell into a trance and saw him there, speaking to me. "Make haste," he said, "and leave Jerusalem without delay, for they will not accept your teaching about me." . . . "Go, for I am sending you far away to the Gentiles",'

words which roused afresh the fury of the mob. It evidently needed a special vision and revelation to convince St Paul that the Gospel was for the Gentiles as well as for the Jews. In the early years of his apostleship he had simply preached in the synagogues and 'confounded the Jews'; after this vision he had to prepare himself to preach to the Gentiles, who knew not the Scriptures.

These two visions were 'Christologies'—visions of Christ, and their validity was completely attested by their fruits, yet the writers and thinkers of the early Christian centuries placed more emphasis on the experience described by St Paul, almost against his will, and, as it were out of sheer necessity, in 2 Corinthians 12: 1–5:

> I will come to visions and revelations of the Lord. I knew a man in Christ above fourteen years ago (whether in the body, I cannot tell; or whether out of the body, I cannot tell: God knoweth); such an one caught up to the third heaven. And I knew such a man (whether in the body, or out of the body, I cannot tell: God knoweth); how that he was caught up into paradise, and heard unspeakable words, which it is not lawful for a man to utter. Of such an one will I glory; yet of myself I will not glory, but in mine infirmities (A.V.).

(I have here quoted from the Authorised Version because the N.E.B. translates 'en Christo' as 'Christian', which in this particular context is somewhat unfortunate.)

This was not a 'Christology' in the same sense as the vision before Damascus: it was a 'mystical rapture'—the only one mentioned by the Apostle, and therefore of peculiar interest. Here the raptures of the great Christian mystics have their scriptural sanction. This rapture proved that St Paul was no whit behind the other Apostles who had known the Lord 'in the flesh' (12: 11); it established the true value and authenticity of his apostolate. He goes on to point out that the true marks of an apostle were there, in the work he did among them which 'was attended by signs, marvels and miracles' (12: 12). We are also told in Acts that

> through Paul God worked miracles of an unusual kind: when handkerchiefs and scarves which had been in contact with his skin were carried to the sick, they were rid of their diseases and the evil spirits came out of them (Acts 19: 11, 12).

There is an important point to be noted here. This rapture was connected quite clearly with St Paul's apostolic mission: it gave him confidence and enabled him to preach the Gospel with complete assurance, for here he was drawn into very close union with Christ; it gave him insight into the mysteries of the Faith. Consequently, we must conclude that 'rapture' is in no sense a necessary part of the ordinary Christian life, or, for that matter, of the life of the Church as a whole. This is important, for it distinguishes it quite definitely from the mysticism of the 'mystery-religions' of that time, whose ultimate aim and object was the mystical experience *in itself*, as it is, indeed, among many primitive peoples, for mystical experience is universal. St Paul gives no directions in his writings as to how rapture is to be attained, or what disciplines are to be undertaken with a view to its attainment: nor could he, since he was 'caught up', and did not 'raise himself'. Nowhere, either, does he express a desire for a repetition of this experience. Nevertheless, though 'rapture' forms no part of the ideal for every Christian, we must believe from this passage in Corinthians that it is an authentic part of the full Christian mystical life. The value of exceptional mystical experiences, it is well to remember, is of importance primarily for the Church and humanity as a whole rather than for the individual. The world would be very much the poorer without her saints and mystics, who have known by experience the wonder of the love of God, but for the ordinary Christian the ideal is perfection of charity and not mystical experience, which is given by God when and where he wills and sees fit, often to the most unlikely subjects. This is apparent if we think, for instance, of a simple peasant child like Bernadette of Lourdes and her visions, which have proved so fruitful. Naturally it is true that mystical experience, where it is genuine, cannot but lead to a perfecting of the life of charity, since it means union with God who is Love.

'I know a man *in* Christ,' says St Paul: that is, a man no longer in the state in which man, since the Fall, has lived outside the Garden of Eden, but *in* the second Adam, who has once more opened paradise to man.

Caught up into the third . . . Caught up into Paradise.

There is some uncertainty as to whether St Paul is here speaking of two separate and distinct raptures, or whether both descriptions—'the third heaven' and 'Paradise'— apply to the same place, and describe one experience. Most of the Fathers of the Early Church accepted the latter

explanation, and it is the more generally accepted interpretation. Here, however, we will think of the implications
of each separately.

Dom Anselm Stolz sees in this mention of a 'third
heaven' an allusion to a Stoical conception according to
which souls find themselves, at their departure from this
life, in the 'zone of fire' of the third spiritual heaven.[1]
This would certainly support the view that the Stoic teaching
had some influence on the thought of St Paul, but it also
has a very close resemblance to the implications of being
'caught up into Paradise' in mystical theology. God
brought Adam, whom he had created outside the garden,
into the Garden of Eden in order that he might both learn
to contemplate God, and to care for the Garden. Work,
we may note in passing, is not the punishment meted out
to man after the Fall; man was meant to work, but the
penalty for sin lay in the fact that the work was fruitless—
the land brought forth thorns and thistles (Gen. 3: 18).
The only way in which man in those earliest days of his life
on earth could know God was in the interior of his soul:
there were no other means of conveying to him this knowledge. Through the Fall man lost this power of contemplation: he could no longer hear the 'still, small voice of God'
speaking within. Having turned away from God (Gen.
3: 10), he could no longer live in the Garden of God. He
was cast out, and cherubim and a flaming sword were placed
to guard the approach to the Tree of Life in the Garden
(Gen. 3: 24). Henceforth humanity, in order to enter
Paradise, must pass through the flame, the fire of purification. Thus the teaching of St John of the Cross that the
way to the most perfect union with God is through the

[1] A. Stolz: *Theologie de la Mystique*, p. 27.

'dark night of loving fire' (Dark Night, Bk. 2, xii) is firmly founded on scripture, as was so much of his spiritual teaching. Mystical union with God is identified with the joys of Paradise.

Philo rejected all material ideas of a Garden of Paradise: he thought of paradise as the interior of the soul, and of the trees as the virtues. St Ambrose, who wrote a whole treatise on Paradise, to a very great extent followed this interpretation:

> Paradise is the soul in which are planted the virtues [he wrote] and where the Tree of Life, that is Wisdom, is also to be found.[1]

Yet in his introduction to De Paradiso he remarked that St Paul evidently thought of the paradise of Adam as being always in existence, thus following the teaching of St Irenaeus. Many early writers located paradise in this world. St Isidore of Seville, in the seventh century, thought that it must be in Asia, on the Indian or Assyrian coast. St Thomas Aquinas dealt with this idea in his Summa, and did not deny its existence on this earth. He thought paradise was separated from the inhabited world by high mountains, vast oceans and wild regions, and believed it to be inaccessible to man. He thought that Enoch and Elias, since they had been translated, dwelt in paradise. These ideas may actually have had their origin in ancient mythical thought connected with the gods and the departed. Even Christopher Columbus, great discoverer as he was, still believed, as a good Catholic, in an earthly paradise, and longed above all to find it.

The early Church maintained that paradise remained

[1] De. Para., 2, C.S.E.L. 267.18.

closed to humankind till the death of Christ. One Good Friday, St John Chrysostom cried:

> Now God has opened paradise which had been closed for five thousand years; today, at this very hour, he led the robber into it, thus accomplishing a double work: opening paradise and then bringing the robber into it.[1]

The Church, we may note in passing, as she celebrates her festivals, enters into the absolute contemporaneousness of the events of salvation: it is always 'today', because these events are rooted both in time and in eternity, and therefore they partake of both: they are shown forth here, in this world, within 'time', yet because they are the works of God and partake of his 'timelessness' they, too, are timeless.

The Fathers taught that the way of salvation brought men first to paradise, but that since the grace of Christ far surpasses that of Adam paradise cannot be the final state of the redeemed. St Ambrose, though he spoke of paradise as a part of heaven, held it to be, as it were, the foundation on which the kingdom of heaven was built, and from which the elect would rise, each according to his merits, to their own place.[2] Theophylacte, in the eleventh century, protested against confusing the two ideas of paradise and the kingdom of heaven, for he pointed out that 'Eye hath not seen, nor ear heard, neither have entered into the heart of man the things God hath prepared for them that love him', whereas, he maintained, man *has* seen the joys of paradise, and his ear has heard them.[3]

In his rapture St Paul was caught up above this sinful world, not only into the 'paradise' of Adam, but 'into

[1] *De Croce et latrone. hom.* 1, n. 2, P.G. 49, 401.
[2] Ep. 71, 8, P.L. 16.
[3] *In Lucam.* c. 23, *de Ph. Strauch*, 1881, p. 65.

Christ', something far surpassing the original earthly paradise. His experience of 'vision' followed by 'rapture'
appears again in that of one of the early martyrs—St
Perpetua—whose own account of one of her last visions
has come down to us in words written on the eve of her
martyrdom. Her brother, imprisoned with her, was convinced that she was a 'peculiar favourite of heaven' and
asked her to pray that God would reveal to her whether or
not their imprisonment would end in martyrdom. She tells
us that in her vision she saw a ladder with a dragon at its
foot, but though the dragon was so fierce she had no fear
that it would bite her, so great was her trust in Jesus
Christ:

> And the dragon, as if afraid of me, gently lifted his head
> from under the ladder, and I, having got upon the first
> step, set my foot upon his head. Thus I mounted to the
> top, and there I saw a garden of an immense space, and in
> the middle of it a tall man sitting down dressed like a
> shepherd, having white hair. He was milking his sheep,
> surrounded by many thousands of persons clad in white.
> He called me by my name, bid me welcome, and gave me
> some curds made of the milk which he had drawn: I put my
> hands together and took and ate them; and they that were
> present said alone, Amen. The noise awaked me, chew-
> ing something very sweet.

She adds simply that when she related this to her brother
they both concluded that they should suffer death. Here
many points in the conception of paradise come together:
mastery over the animals, the garden, food taken from the
hand of Christ, the heavenly banquet.

It is recounted of St Perpetua that, having been torn by
a wild bull during her martyrdom, she appeared to have
known nothing about it, and asked when she was to have

her tussle with the wild cow. To her surprise she was told that it was all over and would not believe it till she looked down and saw her torn body and bleeding wounds.

'Where was she when assaulted?' cried St Augustine, referring to this incident, 'and torn by so furious a wild beast, without feeling her wounds, and when after that furious combat, she asked when it would begin? What did she not to see what all the world saw? What did she enjoy who did not feel such pain? By what love, by what vision, by what potion was she so transported out of herself, and as it were divinely inebriated, to seem without feeling in a mortal body?'

Was she not 'caught up into paradise' as St Paul had been? Rapt and blissful in the love of Christ, she endured her tortures bathed in joy, upheld by him to whom she had given her whole heart and soul.

4

The Development of
St Paul's Mystical Teaching

ST PAUL'S teaching on our life 'in Christ' develops gradually in his Epistles, beginning with a slight hint in Thessalonians:

This is what God in Christ wills for you (1 Thess. 5: 18).

and coming to its full expression in the Epistles of the Captivity. Various reasons have been suggested for this gradual development of his mystical thought. It may be due, in part, to the slow fading out of the expectation of Christ's immediate return, or, on the other hand, it may be simply the natural process of striving after a more perfect expression of that which was revealed to the saint in vision. All vital and living ideas which are placed as 'seeds' in the human mind by God take time to grow and expand and come to their full fruition. Only very slowly can our limited human intelligence grasp and lay hold of the deep things of God. Cardinal Newman, who spent many years of his life working out his theory of the development of doctrine and of ideas in general, and whose thought on this subject is scattered throughout his writings, showed clearly that ideas only come to their full fruition when they have been subjected to all the various processes of criticism and disapproval, when they have been battered upon by many minds, when they have had to be upheld in face of opposition. Only thus can any great thought come to its fullest development. The very life of true development is realising. The more truly 'living' any idea is the more varied are its aspects, and therefore the mind can only by degrees unfold its contents. This must certainly have been true of St Paul's mystical doctrine of life 'in Christ Jesus'. His writings are not easy to understand: they abound in allusions to the Old Testament, and the Septuagint at that, and they are poured out of the living, passionate heart of one who had been taken captive by Christ. Perhaps this has seldom been more forcefully and beautifully brought out than in Myer's poem on St Paul:

> Christ's, only Christ's, be this my lifelong story;
> Christ's, only Christ's, my one and only joy.

Thought, after all, is the outcome of the whole of a man's being, the expression of all the manifold facets of that nature which he has developed out of the original endowment bestowed upon him at birth. If genius lies supremely not in lucidity of thought but in the capacity for experiencing intensely, then St Paul certainly possessed this primary characteristic of genius, and his thoughts are not always lucidly expressed or easily understood.

Though the immediate source of St Paul's teaching on 'en Christo' must be ascribed to his own mystical experience, we must also take account of the background of his thought, for this was the material he had to use in developing his doctrine. Because this background was so rich, so perfectly adapted to express his experience in ways that would be most widely understood, he was an instrument ready to God's hand. In him many lines of development converged. He was thoroughly versed in the Hebrew Scriptures with their teaching on the one 'living God', whose hand had guided his people through the centuries, and who had spoken through the great mystics and prophets of the Old Testament. On the other hand, he was a Jew of Tarsus, and Tarsus was the centre of Stoicism. As a Jew of the Dispersion he would daily have come in contact with Greek culture, and the flexible Greek language which he knew so well was an instrument perfectly adapted to interpret the East to the West. His Bible was the Greek Septuagint, and though his thought is usually Hebraic the Greek influence must surely have penetrated, however unconsciously, into his being. When he was called to be the 'Apostle of the Gentiles' he would undoubtedly have studied the Jewish Scriptures afresh in the light of this revelation, and would also have considered the best elements in Stoicism in order to help him to preach the Gospel in the way these Gentiles would best understand.

For St Paul, Christianity was Christ—Christ crucified and risen—the ever-present personal Saviour. His preaching was not in any words of human wisdom or rhetoric, but simply of Christ and him crucified:

> Christ did not send me to baptize, but to proclaim the Gospel; and to do it without relying on the language of worldly wisdom, so that the fact of Christ on his cross might have full weight . . . Jews call for miracles, Greeks look for wisdom; but we proclaim Christ—yes, Christ nailed to the cross; and though it is a stumbling-block to Jews and folly to Greeks, yet to those who have heard his call, Jews and Greeks alike, he is the power of God and the wisdom of God (1 Cor. 1 : 22–24).

Again he cries to the Corinthians:

I resolved that while I was with you I would think of nothing but Jesus Christ—Christ nailed to the cross (1 Cor. 2: 2).

Writing to the Galatians he says:

God forbid that I should glory, save in the cross of our Lord Jesus Christ, by whom the world is crucified to me, and I unto the world (Gal. 6: 14).

We should do well sometimes to ask ourselves why St Paul so gloried in the Cross of Christ—the Cross of shame, which to him contained so supreme a mystery and wonder. There are manifold reasons, for here, hidden in that Cross of Christ, lies the deepest mystery and wonder of the universe. We will try, as we go on, to bring out some of these points, but often the answer must be given out of the depths of our own hearts, of our own suffering and our own need. The early Christians were fascinated by this mystery which, in the lowliest and simplest form, veiled so great a wonder, and the early Fathers loved to dwell on the thought of the 'hiddenness' of God. One of the oldest Christian hymns expresses this thought:

The earth shook . . . the whole creation was amazed, marvelling, and saying, 'What new mystery, then, is this?
. . .
The Invisible One is seen, and is not ashamed;
the Incomprehensible is laid hold upon, and is not indignant
. . .
The Impassible suffereth, and doth not avenge;
the Immortal dieth, and answereth not a word . . .
What new mystery is this? (*Melito of Sardis*, fr. 13).

The early Christian mystics saw the form of the Cross imprinted on the whole of creation, in the form of everyday things and in the starry firmament. For St Irenaeus the

Cross was the recapitulation of all cosmic and biblical history. In a passage which has become one of the best-known texts on the mystery of the Cross he wrote:

> Now seeing that he is the Word of God Almighty, who in unseen wise in our midst is universally extended in all the world, and encompasses its length and breadth and height and depth—for by the Word of God the whole universe is ordered and disposed—in it is crucified the Son of God, inscribed crosswise upon it all: for it is right that he, being made visible, should set upon all things visible the sharing of his Cross, that he might show his operation on visible things through the visible form.   For he it is who illumines the height that is the heavens; and encompasses the deep that is beneath the earth; and stretches and spreads out the length from east to west; and steers across the breadth of north and south; summoning all that are scattered in every quarter to the knowledge of the Father (*Epideixis*, I, 34).

The Cross is thus a symbol of something vast and unknown —a mystery.[1]

If we compare some of the earlier verses of the First Epistle to the Corinthians with the first chapter of Ephesians we see how the thoughts so fully developed in the later Epistle are already present in the earlier one.

> I am always thanking God for you.   I thank him for the grace given to you *in* Christ Jesus.   I thank him for all the enrichment that has come to you *in* Christ.   You possess full knowledge and you can give full expression to it, because in you the evidence for the truth of Christ has found full confirmation. . . . It is God himself who has called you to share in the life of his Son Jesus Christ our Lord; and God keeps faith (1 Cor. 1: 4f.).

[1] Plato had written in the *Timaeus* of the world soul revealed in the celestial X, and as early a writer as Justin related this passage in Plato to the Son of God.   Though he only suggests this briefly, there can be no doubt that he was already familiar with the idea.

You are *in* Christ Jesus by God's act; for God has made him our wisdom (1 Cor. 1: 30).

Here, following the Greek Fathers, some exegetes give the verb 'to be' the sense of 'to exist', so we may translate this: 'You exist in Christ.' There, in Corinthians, St Paul leaves it, but the seeds of the ideas are there, and they meet us again in the Epistle to the Ephesians (Eph. 1: 3ff.).

In the Epistle to the Romans, written about a year after 1 Corinthians, the thought of the 'mystery' is more fully developed. The idea which was to reappear later in Ephesians that our redemption in Christ, foretold in ancient times, is now fulfilled, is worked out in Romans 3: 21–26. All are justified by God's free grace alone, through his 'act' of liberation in the Person of Christ Jesus. All the thoughts of this great passage: the idea of election and glory and purification; the thought of the calling both of Jews and Gentiles *in* Christ, are elements in the 'mystery' which has now been revealed. Here we find St Paul struggling with the immensity of the message he was called to proclaim. In chapters 9 to 11 he deals with the strange fact that the Gentiles have entered into that great heritage which had been prepared for the children of promise, and suddenly there breaks from him a cry of marvelling wonder:

O depth of wealth, wisdom and knowledge in God! How unsearchable are his judgments and his ways past finding out (Rom. 11: 33).

This Epistle also contains that wonderful passage which is surely one of the most beautiful in all the Scriptures, and which the N.E.B. renders with great power:

Then what can separate us from the love of Christ? Can affliction or hardship? Can persecution, hunger, nakedness, peril or sword? . . . I am convinced that there is nothing in death or life, in the realm of spirits or superhuman powers, in the world as it is or the world as it shall be, in forces of the universe, in heights or depths—nothing in all creation that can separate us from the love of God in Christ Jesus our Lord (Rom. 8: 35–39).

'The knowledge of Christ is the light shining in darkness,' says St Paul in the Second Epistle to the Corinthians (4:6). This light which shines in the hearts of Christians must manifest itself in outward behaviour: the ministers of Christ, above all, must prove themselves as ministers of God in the midst of suffering and affliction, in much patience by knowledge, by long-suffering, by kindness, by love unfeigned:

as sorrowful, yet always rejoicing; as poor, yet making many rich; as having nothing and yet possessing all things (2 Cor. 6: 10).

In this thought of patience and love in the midst of afflictions there rings the true note of primitive Christian thinking. We find it again in the First Epistle of St Peter, which may contain some of the very earliest teaching in the New Testament. This was *the* way in which Christ's followers could obey his injunction to take up their cross and follow after him.

Though traditionally the Pauline authorship of Ephesians has never been questioned, in recent years certain doubts have been raised as to its authenticity. The Epistle is more general than any other, it is not addressed to the peculiar needs of any particular church, it has none of the personal greetings which we find in the other Epistles. The words 'to the Ephesians' are not found in all the early manuscripts: there is simply a space. It may have been a circular letter—an encyclical—and that would account for most of these facts. However, as far as the teaching on our life of union with Christ is concerned this matter of authorship or the destination of the letter is of little account, especially if we bear in mind the fact that all ideas, if they are true and 'living', must go on developing. If, as some scholars think, Ephesians was not written by St Paul, then it must have been written by one of his followers who had so clearly grasped his doctrine that he was able to express what St Paul had gradually been trying to formulate more perfectly than the Apostle himself. Here, certainly, is the full flowering of the Pauline mystical teaching. Its date could hardly have been later than A.D. 65.

In Ephesians, St Paul returns to the thought of the great 'mystery' hid from other generations, but now made known: that the Gentiles should be partakers of the Gospel. For one brought up as a Hebrew of the Hebrews this was a tremendous fact to grasp. A wall of separation had been built up between the Jews and the Gentiles for centuries, and, after years of conflict, there was deep prejudice to be overcome. In the light of this fresh revelation that the Gentiles were to share in the new life brought by Christ, St Paul must have had to study the Scriptures afresh, reading them in this new light. Nevertheless here, as in all his Epistles, he speaks to us directly, in his impassioned language, as a man of the first century, and of all the New Testament writers it is he who uses the word 'mystery' by far the most frequently. Now this word 'mystery', 'μυστήριον' or 'μυστήρια', was in very frequent use in the Mediterranean world of his day. The Greek 'mysteries' were celebrated throughout the regions St Paul visited, in Alexandria, Rome and Asia Minor, but above all at Eleusis,

which lay very near Athens, where he found the altar to the
'unknown God'.   Therefore he who taught the 'mystery
of Christ' must have been very familiar with the pre-
Christian usage of the word.   To the Ephesians to whom he
wrote the word would certainly have suggested the
'mystery cults' which were so well known among them.
Clearly in this Epistle the Apostle juxtaposes to the other
'mysteries' the 'mystery of Christ'—the mystery of God
Who created all things—which 'in other generations was
not known to the sons of men, as it is now revealed to his
holy apostles and prophets by the Spirit' (Eph. 3: 5).   In
the Greek Septuagint, the Bible used by St Paul, the word
means 'the secret plan of the king'.   To the Gentile
Christians at Ephesus he wrote:

> Having made known to us the mystery of his will, according
> to his good pleasure which he hath purposed in himself;
> that in the dispensation of the fulness of times he might
> gather together in one all things in Christ, both which are in
> heaven, and which are on earth (Eph. 1: 9, 10).

In the first two chapters he gathers up many thoughts on
our life 'in Christ': from the foundation of the world God
has chosen us in him, having predestinated us to the adoption of children by Jesus Christ to himself, to the praise
of the glory of his grace, 'wherein he hath made us accepted
to the beloved'; he has made known the mystery of his will
to gather up all things 'in Christ'; we are created 'in
Christ' to good works; by his death Christ has broken down
the middle wall of partition between Jew and Gentile,
making both one: he who is our peace.   By his blood-
shedding Jesus Christ has made a new treaty of peace between the opposing sections of humanity: Jew and Gentile.
He has taken our common humanity so that 'in him' all

flesh, that is, all humanity, should find its meeting-point:

> He is himself our peace (Eph. 2: 14).

The emphasis is on the pronoun: *he* in his own person is our peace. Here the thought comes very close to that of St John. The Gentiles are now to share all the privileges of the Jews; they too, are of the household of God, built on the foundation of the Apostles and Prophets, of which Jesus Christ is the foundation-stone, or keystone. They are builded together for an habitation of God.

In the third chapter St Paul becomes personal: 'I, the prisoner of Jesus Christ.' There follows a fresh train of thought: God's revelation to himself. He echoes many of the thoughts of the first two chapters, but

> By revelation . . . his secret was made known to me (3: 3).

Though in the Second Epistle to the Corinthians he had declared that he was 'no whit behind the very chiefest of the Apostles' (11: 5), here he says that he is 'less than the least of all saints', and yet God has given him this marvellous grace of being allowed to penetrate into his mysterious purpose. St Paul is convinced that he has been given an insight into God's eternal purpose; the very purpose of creation itself, which has only now been revealed, and is manifest to the whole universe, justifying God's dealings with men. He is sure that he is in possession of the very secret of the Creator himself, and in the strength of this conviction he attempts a complete philosophy of history: something that had never before been attempted. He declares that an unceasing purpose runs through all the ages, and that he, Paul, has been entrusted with the knowledge of this purpose, so that he can, as it were, flash a torch of light across the darkness of this world, to illuminate the past, the present and the future.   Though the thought that Jews and Gentiles are all to be 'one in Christ' is to him a great mystery and wonder, yet *the* great wonder is that which he calls 'the unfathomable riches of Christ' (Eph. 3: 9).   He prays that those to whom he writes, whoever they may be, may be 'strengthened', that they may be able to grasp, with all God's people,

> what is the breadth and length and height and depth of the love of Christ, and to know it, though it is beyond knowledge (3: 18, 19).

The Greek word here used for 'strengthened'—'ἐξισχύσητε' is found nowhere else in the New Testament, and suggests the difficulty of the task, which calls for all their strength. Though 'rooted and grounded' in Christ by baptism, they must never cease to reach up and out that they may be able by God's grace to grasp in some measure the depths of the love of God—that unspeakable wonder: unplumbed, unplumbable.   Here, at last, we have the full expression of what 'life in Christ' really meant for St Paul.   Here is that note of the utterly mysterious and incomprehensible content of this life—this 'new life' into which we are brought 'in Christ'.   Those familiar with the mystical aspirations of the Greek 'mystes' and the spiritual experiences which alone can account for the widespread popularity of the 'Mysteries', would surely have seen here the fulfilment of their deepest spiritual desires.

St Paul goes on to show what this new life in Christ is to be, for though he takes us up into the heights his feet are always firmly on the ground: the moral and ethical content of his message is never lost sight of for very long:

Be ye humble always and gentle, and patient too. Be
forbearing one with another and charitable. Spare no
effort to make fast the bands of peace (Eph. 4: 2, 3).

There are no heroics here, no flights of rapture, but that
showing forth of the true Christian 'agape' which he had
sung so beautifully in the first Epistle to the Corinthians
(ch. 13).

We need not dwell here on the great passage in Ephesians
4: 1–16, for it is possibly one of the most familiar in the
New Testament, summing up as it does the whole content
of the Faith, yet there is one point that calls for some com-
ment, since it is open to different interpretations.

Now, the word 'ascended' implies that he also descended to
the lowest level, down to the very earth (Eph. 4: 9 in
N.E.B.).

This rendering makes the 'descending' apply to the 'keno-
sis', the 'self-emptying' of the Son of God at the incarnation,
a thought developed in Philippians 2: 5–11.   On the other
hand, the rendering of the Authorised Version:

Now that he ascended, what is it but that he also descended
first into the lower parts of the earth?   He that descended is
the same also that ascended far above all heavens, that he
might fill all things,

is more in keeping with the ancient three-dimensional conceptions: Heaven, earth and hell, and gives us the thought
of the 'breaking through the planes' that he might fill all
things, and bring us into the captivity of his love, which we
find again in Colossians (1: 19, 20).

The tremendous scope of St Paul's thought is brought out
in these later Epistles:

Finally then, find your strength in the Lord, in his mighty
power.   Put on the whole armour which God provides,

so that you may be able to stand firm against the devices of the devil. For our fight is not against human foes, but against cosmic powers, against the authorities and potentates of this dark world, against the superhuman forces of evil in the heavens (Eph. 6: 10–12).

We meet the same idea in Colossians, where St Paul speaks of the heavenly kingdom into which we are brought 'in Christ':

Giving thanks unto the Father, which hath made us meet to be partakers of the inheritance of the saints in light: Who hath delivered us from the power of darkness, and hath translated us into the kingdom of his dear Son (Col. 1: 12, 13).

In Philippians, that undoubtedly Pauline Epistle, come those words which seem to sum up the whole of St Paul's life:

All I can say is this: forgetting what is behind me, and reaching out to that which lies ahead, I press towards the goal to win the prize which is God's call to the life above, in Christ Jesus . . . We are citizens of heaven, and from heaven we expect our deliverer to come, the Lord Jesus Christ . . . The Lord is near; have no anxiety, but in everything make your requests known to God in prayer and petition with thanksgiving. Then the peace of God, which is beyond our utmost understanding, will guard over your hearts and your thoughts, in Christ Jesus (Phil. 3: 13, 14, 20; 4: 6, 7).

We are to fill our minds with all that is just and pure and noble and lovable; we are to set our hearts on that which is above, for, as Christians, our 'life is hid with Christ in God' (Col. 3: 3). Then, at the last, when Christ, 'who is our life', shall appear, we too shall appear with him in glory.

5

Some Subordinate Images

Though 'en Christo' is undoubtedly the fundamental expression of St Paul's mystical thought, he also used other images to describe the life of union with Christ. His great mind laid hold of many and varied aspects of his fundamental concept, or what we may call his 'master-image'. We have seen that for the Apostle the expressions 'in Christ' and 'Christ in us' seem to have been practically identical: he uses them almost interchangeably. The thought of our dwelling in Christ and his dwelling in us were simply different ways of saying the same thing; slightly different aspects of the one great reality.

Sometimes St Paul uses the formula 'in the Holy Spirit', which we actually find nineteen times in his Epistles. Deissmann saw in this the same fundamental notion as 'in Christ', and thought it really meant 'in Christ who is the Spirit'. On this question there are several points to be made clear. In the first place, when St Paul speaks of being 'in Christ' he is always referring to salvation *as such*:

> When anyone is united to Christ, there is a new world (or a new creation), the old order has gone, a new order has already begun (2 Cor. 5: 17).

When he uses 'in the Spirit' he is thinking rather of the conduct of Christians in contrast to the conduct of the natural man in his fallen state. For instance, in Romans 8 : 1 he says:

> In Christ Jesus the life-giving law of the Spirit has set you free from the law of sin and death,

and again in Galatians:

> If you are guided by the Spirit you will not fulfil the desires of your lower nature. That nature sets its desires against the Spirit, while the Spirit fights against it. They are in conflict with one another, so that what you will to do you cannot do. But if you are led by the Spirit, you are not under the Law (Gal. 5: 16–18).

> Those who belong to Christ have crucified the lower nature with its passions and desires. If the Spirit is the source of our life, let the Spirit also direct our course (Gal. 5: 24, 25).

In Romans, St Paul says much about the Spirit of God and the Spirit of Christ, and we must try to understand what the import of these phrases is. The work of the Holy Spirit in the Church is so important that it is vital for us to realise what St Paul meant by these expressions. St Paul never speaks of the Church, or the 'Body', as a prolongation of the Spirit. His constant teaching is that we only have this relationship with Christ, and in Christ with the Son of God: in him, and in him alone, the whole of humanity has access to the whole of the divinity. The Second Person of the Blessed Trinity has, through his Incarnation, a very special and peculiar union with our humanity 'by incommunicable property of personal union' (Pearson, quoted by Liddon in his Bampton Lectures, p. 261). For St Paul the Holy Spirit is always the Spirit of Christ, and his activity in the Church is practically identical with that of the Risen Christ himself. It is the

Spirit of the Risen and Ascended Lord working in his Church. This, as Professor Lampe has pointed out,[1] is the difference between the hope of the outpouring of the Spirit in the Old Testament, and its actual fulfilment, for the Spirit bestowed on the Church is the Spirit of Jesus. The idea of the Spirit in the earlier New Testament writings is that of the power and presence of the ascended Jesus in the eternal Kingdom of God energising within time in his Body the Church. The Spirit can now work within the 'new creation' in a way that was not possible before Jesus was glorified. The Early Church confined the operation of the Holy Spirit strictly to the Redeemed, while emphasising the fact of the active relation to Christ, the eternal Word of God, to all men and all creatures.

In biblical thought God exerting influence is the Spirit of God. In the Old Testament the thought is of 'wind' or 'breath': invisible, but a very real energy producing quite definite effects; an influence that is felt. God's influence is dynamic: it gives life, strength and power. In St Paul's teaching the Spirit of God was the Spirit of Jesus:

> You are on a spiritual level, if only God's Spirit dwells within you; and if a man does not possess the Spirit of Christ, he is no Christian (Rom. 8: 9).

In Corinthians he speaks of some of the rather spectacular 'gifts' of the Spirit which manifested themselves in apostolic days, but he is not carried away by them:

> All these gifts are the work of one and the same Spirit, distributing them separately to each individual at will. For Christ is like a single body with many limbs and organs, which, many as they are, together make up one body (1 Cor. 12: 11, 12).

[1] G. W. H. Lampe: *The Seal of the Spirit*, pp. 49, 50.

But, he goes on to say 'If I am without love, I am a sounding brass or a tinkling cymbal' (13 : 1).

The lasting effects produced by the Holy Spirit are given in Galatians:

> love, joy, peace, kindness, goodness, fidelity, gentleness and self-control (Gal. 5: 22).

In Philippians he shows what our common life 'in Christ' is to be:

> If this produces anything to stir the heart, any loving consolation, any sharing of the Spirit, any warmth of affection or compassion, fill up my cup of joy by thinking and feeling alike, with the same love for one another, the same turn of mind, and a common care for unity . . . Let your bearing towards one another arise out of your life in Christ Jesus (Phil. 2: 1ff.).

In the Greater Epistles we see the gradual formation of the metaphor of the 'Body'. This is more fully developed in the Epistles of the Captivity. It is a distinctively Pauline conception, which cannot claim to be based directly on the teaching of Jesus himself, as was his 'en Christo', though it is a perfectly legitimate development, and one of great value. In Ephesians the exalted Christ is 'supreme head to the Church, which is his body, the fullness of him that filleth all in all.' There are many versions of this passage, all with slightly different emphases. In Colossians he is 'the head of the body the Church' quite simply. Christ is the *Head* of the Church because he is God, and therefore it is clear that the unity of the members of the Church with Christ is more intimate than their unity among themselves, since 'the former is the cause of the latter'.[1]

Much thought has been given in recent years to the con-

[1] E. Mersch: op. cit., p. 109.

cept of the Church as the Body of Christ, but while revival of interest in Christ's Body in this world is to be welcomed, there are certain points on which we must exercise some caution. The Church *is* the Body of Christ in this world: without her there would have been no Christian Faith; she is the expression of the Christlife in time and space. Nevertheless she is composed of frail and erring human beings, and therefore to emphasise the fact that 'to be "in Christ" is simply to be incorporated into the Church, which is his Body, the New Israel',[1] though true as far as it goes, may be extremely misleading. Again, to say that for St Paul and St John to be 'in Christ' or Christ being 'in us' was simply 'the familiar language in which Hebrews for centuries expressed their awareness of the solidarity of the human race—of the relations of persons with persons', that the 'many can be, indeed, are "one" '[2] is inadequate: it leaves out that which is essential, the 'vertical' relationship to Christ the Lord, who is the *Head* of the Body. As we have already seen, St Paul never says the Church *is* Christ, or that *we* are Christ. In his study of Ephesians, Dr Armitage Robinson put this point very clearly:

That the 'one Spirit' is ultimately indistinguishable from the personal Holy Spirit is true, just as in the same way the 'one body' is indistinguishable from the Body of Christ: but we could not in either case substitute the one term for the other without obscuring the Apostle's meaning (p. 162).

There are two schools of thought as to the exact function of the Church. There is the 'active' interpretation and the 'passive' one. The former was supported by Dr Armitage Robinson and other scholars, and teaches that the Church

---

[1] N. Clarke: *An Approach to the Theology of the Sacraments*, p. 24.
[2] A. Richardson: *Introduction to the Theology of the New Testament*, p. 250.

is here to *fufil* Christ, to give him his final perfection. The second, the 'passive' interpretation, upheld by Dr Lightfoot and others, holds that the Church does not add anything to Christ, but simply receives from him, and is here to contain the fullness of his power and redemptive riches. The Church is filled with the riches of Christ; she exists in order to contain him. She is also the Body of Christ *redeeming us*, joined to Christ in one moment of history, the 'instant of our redemption'.[1]

In Ephesians, too, St Paul speaks of the Church not only as the Body of Christ but also as his 'Bride', which is a 'great mystery'. He compares it with the earthly marriage union:

> Husbands, love your wives, as Christ also loved the Church and gave himself for it (5: 25).

The Church's union with Christ is so close that the earthly marriage union is but a pale reflection of it. This union of Christ with his followers and with his Church is thus the fulfilment of the Old Testament 'nuptial' motif. Yet in the last resort the application must be made individually, since each soul must be united directly with the 'Whole' with 'Omega' in faith and love, which can only exist in the 'body' through the 'individual':

> Thus it is that (in the words of Scripture) 'a man shall leave his father and mother and shall be joined to his wife, and the two shall become one single body'. It is a great truth that is hidden here. I for my part refer it to Christ and to the Church, but it also applies individually (Eph. 5: 31–33).

[1] 'To define the Church as the Body of Christ is to define her incompletely: she is the body of Christ redeeming us, joined to our Saviour in one special moment of history, in the instant of our Redemption. She is the body of Christ in the act of his death and resurrection. The identification is dynamic as well as existential; for it is effected by participation in the same action in a shared being.' (F. X. Durrwell: *The Resurrection*, p. 222.)

The distinction between Christ and his Church must be maintained, as well as the distinction between Christ and the individual Christian. To forget this is to leave out of our thoughts that element of 'mystery' which was so distinctive of St Paul's mysticism. Christ is above all and embraces us all in himself; we are not 'absorbed' in him, yet, though we are 'in him' our being is not blended with his; it is enfolded in him. Without any loss to himself—God and Man—he can give to each one of us a share in his humanity, and he himself 'shareth our infirmities'. No mere external relation, such as being members of his visible Body, 'can exhaust the inwardness of the words "*in* Christ" '. At first sight, as Dr Pusey pointed out many years ago, it hardly seems to convey more than that our blessings come to us through him, yet it

> opens up a greater fullness of mystery to those who would penetrate below the surface, and would wish to see what they may see—the hidden mystery of our union with Christ, and of the reality of our dwelling in him, and he in us (E. B. Pusey: *The Doctrine of Holy Baptism*, p. 116).

6

The Fourth Gospel : Its Origin and Affinities

THE CONNECTION of the thought of St Paul on our life 'in Christ' with that of St John has been one of the leading questions in the discussion on the New Testament teaching on our union with Christ. Deissmann stated his view quite briefly in the following words:

> The most imposing monument of the genuine understanding of Pauline mysticism is furnished by the Gospel and Epistles of John (*St Paul*, 2nd ed., p. 123).

Commenting on this question Schweitzer made some interesting remarks which cannot, however, be accepted as whole-heartedly as Deissmann's statement. He sees in the Fourth Gospel a Hellenisation of the Pauline teaching, possibly because he emphasised somewhat unduly the purely Jewish background of St Paul. He sees the fundamental difference between the Pauline and Johannine theology to be that in the latter the 'being-in-Christ' is thought of as a 'rebirth', a conception avoided by St Paul, and which Schweitzer regarded as purely Hellenistic. In St John's thought 'being-in-Christ', which in St Paul's writings he declared had not been clearly shown to be a 'being-in-God' is extended to this 'being-in-God'.

> The literary enigma of the writing [he says] is insoluble. We shall never know who the author was . . . but it is

quite clear why he writes . . . it is to show the historic Jesus preaching the mystical doctrine of redemption through being-in-the-Logos-Christ (op. cit., p. 349).

How far may we accept all this?

Dr Schweitzer wrote his book in 1930 and his views, at least at that time, were extremely 'liberal'. He placed the Johannine writer after Ignatius and Justin. Since then the trend of thought has been in the opposite direction. Bishop Gore, in a book published in 1922, had expressed his hope that before long the essentially Palestinian, rather than the Hellenistic origin of the Fourth Gospel, and its high historical witness to the events of Christ's life would soon come to be regarded 'as an assured result of critical enquiry'.[1] Professor Burney in his 'Aramaic Origin of the Fourth Gospel' (1922) suggested that an Aramaic original lay behind the present Greek Gospel of St John, which accounted for the fact that there were more 'Aramaisms' in this Gospel than in any other. Certain passages which are obscure in the Greek he found became perfectly clear when retranslated into Aramaic. He thought the original must have been written in Syrian Antioch, where Aramaic was spoken, possibly between A.D. 75 and 80. The whole of the Fourth Gospel appeared to him to be soaked through and through with Palestinian thought, even the 'Logos' doctrine of the Prologue. Professor O. Cullmann, in an unpublished course given in Strasbourg in 1931–2 pointed out the attachment of the writer to the ideas of St John the Baptist, and G. Kittel, in his famous 'Theologisches

---

[1] 'I am not without hopes that the essentially Palestinian, and not the Hellenistic origin and character of the Fourth Gospel, and its high value as an historical witness both to the events of Our Lord's life and to his teaching, may soon come to be regarded as an "assured result of critical enquiry".' (C. Gore: *Belief in Christ*, p. 107.)

Worterbuch', showed the writer's 'Logos' doctrine to be the pure product of the Biblical teaching of Israel.

In 1934 F. W. Broomfield pleaded for a return to Westcott's view that the writer was none other than St John, the son of Zebedee. He considered that the arguments put forward by modern scholars against this view were not convincing, and thought that the fundamental reason for doubting apostolic authorship was

> the convinction that a person who had known Christ so intimately could not have evolved so exalted a view of his Divinity (*John, Peter and the Fourth Gospel*, p. 187).

He suggested that if we conceive the picture of Christ given in the Fourth Gospel to be true, then it is at least probable that the person who understood him best was the one who came in closest contact with him. He regarded the Johannine Christology as in no way dependent on the Pauline, since there is a noteworthy difference in the standpoints: St Paul's Epistles give the impression that he thought of Christ chiefly in his present state of glory in heaven, and even with regard to his death and resurrection his thought seems to have been mainly directed upon the eternal significance and reality of Christ's work. The Fourth Evangelist, on the other hand, laid particular emphasis on the manifestation of God in the flesh, and might possibly have written his Gospel partly to counteract a dangerous tendency to separate theological speculation from the facts of the Lord's life on earth. Given the religious genius the writer clearly possessed, the Christology of the Fourth Gospel could easily have been evolved, if we take into consideration the impression made by Christ on the other New Testament writers.

In a recent article A. J. B. Higgins has summarised some of the latest results of the research on the Fourth Gospel, which has for long been a subject of vital interest to New Testament scholars.[1] He sees the ultimate basis of the thought of the Gospel to be Jewish and Palestinian—the kind of thought found in the Qumran writings—and he comes to the inescapable conclusion that the traditions used by the Fourth Evangelist are as old and reliable as those of the other Gospels.[2] This Gospel must have been written for readers who already knew the basic truths of Christianity, and could thus understand fuller instruction in the mysteries of their religion; in fact, it has such 'profundities' that only those with a good grounding in the Gospel tradition could possibly appreciate it. Dr J. A. T. Robinson has suggested that since there is no mention of the Gentiles either in the Gospel or the Epistles of St John they were probably written to the Jewish Christians of the Diaspora.[3] Professor Millar Burrows, in a book on the Dead Sea Scrolls published in 1958, said that we now have the real background of the Fourth Gospel in sectarian Judaism, though he realised that this would not go unchallenged.[4]

It is being increasingly realised that the Fourth Gospel is the most Hebraic book in the whole of the New Testament, with the possible exception of the Apocalypse. The whole world it depicts is wholly Jewish, and the word 'Jews'

[1] 'Recent Trends in the Study of the Fourth Gospel' in *Religion in Education*, Summer, 1961.

[2] 'Both go back to the very origins of Palestinian Christianity, and correspond to the two types of Palestinian Judaism.' (O. Cullmann: *Expository Times*, October 1959.)

[3] 'Destination and Purpose of the Fourth Gospel', *N.T. Studies*, 1960, p. 117.

[4] *More Light on the Dead Sea Scrolls*, p. 128.

occurs nearly seventy times.   Yet the writer is not narrowly nationalistic, but immediately introduces the 'cosmic' aspect.   Jesus is 'the real light which enlightens every man' (John 1: 9);   He is 'the Lamb of God . . . who takes away the sin of the world' (1: 29); 'God sent his Son into the world . . . that through him the world might be saved' (3: 17); 'show yourself to the world' (7: 4).

It is true that, as Schweitzer pointed out, this Gospel does speak of 'rebirth': 'Unless a man is born again he cannot see the kingdom of God' (3: 3).   Though this conception was prominent in the Greek mystery religions of the time, and Schweitzer therefore saw in it Hellenistic influences, it was also a term which was perfectly familiar to the Jews of that period in connection with converts to Judaism.   Conversion affected a proselyte's status in two respects: towards God and towards God's people Israel. When received as a proselyte he was as a new-born child with reference to past guilt, and was also cut right off from his family after the flesh: all social relationships had to start anew.

The same may be said with regard to the Johannine 'Logos' doctrine.   Though it has affinities with Philonic thought, there are also differences which make it probable that the writer's dependence on Philo may be limited to the use of the word itself.   Philo of Alexandria used the word 'logos' frequently when speaking of the divine reason which is the intermediary between God and this world, but he also used many personal names to describe this 'Logos', such as 'High Priest', 'First born', and 'Son of God'.   Yet he appears to have thought of the 'Logos' primarily as impersonal, and therefore such an idea as the Logos being 'made flesh' was entirely alien to his thought.

The Fourth Evangelist has some affinities with him, but they must not be exaggerated. In the Fourth Gospel, though there are ideas which have a remarkable resemblance to the Hellenistic Judaism expressed by Philo, the treatment of these ideas is very different, especially when the Evangelist speaks of the 'Word' being incarnate. The Logos of Philo is not the object of faith and love; in the Fourth Gospel it is both Lover and Beloved. To love him, the Incarnate Lord, the Word made Flesh, and to have faith in him, is of the very essence of the knowledge of God which is eternal life.

In the Fourth Gospel, moreover, there is an underlying semitic idiom, though it is written in Greek. We have seen that this led Prof. Burney to postulate an Aramaic original text behind the present Greek Gospel. Obviously the writer knew the phraseology of the Rabbinic Schools, and this brings it into a Jewish environment. He shows knowledge of the sabbath laws (7 : 22–24) and of Rabbinic thought in chapter 9. He must also have had considerable knowledge of the Torah, for he draws contrasts between it and Christianity: the Torah is only the shadow of the heavenly realities which it foreshadowed, and which are ours in Christ. Bread was always regarded as the symbol of the Torah, and St John tells us that the 'true Manna', the true 'Bread from Heaven' was not that given by Moses, but that which God gives us in Jesus Christ (6 : 42).

The whole idea of revelation in the Old Testament was determined by the *word spoken and heard*, as distinct from revelation by vision. This preserved the ontological distance between God and man, and yet affirmed the fact that God, of his own personal choice, approached men in a way they could understand and apprehend, and that he expected from them a response to his approach. For the Hebrew the Word once spoken had a kind of existence of its own. In the Fourth Gospel the word 'logoi', in the plural, is used quite simply of words spoken by Jesus or others, but the singular 'logos' is only used of a 'saying' or 'discourse' or 'statement':

> After his resurrection his disciples recalled what he had said and they believed the scripture and the word (τῷ λόγῳ) that Jesus had spoken (2 : 22).

It was also used collectively for the whole message of Jesus:

> He that heareth my word, and believeth on him that sent me, hath everlasting life (5 : 24) A.V.

and in chapter 15:

> You have already been cleansed by the word that I spoke to you (15 : 3).

It is a word with an underlying meaning. Clearly for the Evangelist the uttered 'word' of Christ, his 'logos', his meaning for the world, is life-giving power by which he gives himself to men. This is definitely a Hebraic conception.

Again, St John uses 'logos' for the Word of God, his self-revelation:

> This testimony was given me by the Father who sent me, although you have never heard his voice, or saw his form. But his word has found no home in you, for you do not believe the one whom he sent (5 : 37).

This is the eternal Truth. Except in the Prologue, where Christ is the Divine Logos, he speaks the word given to him by his Father, and giving life to men:

> The words which I have spoken to you are both spirit and life (6 : 63).

Though here the word 'logos' is not used in the Greek, the meaning comes very close to that of the Prologue.   In the Prologue, however, the thought is cosmic, and the word 'Logos' is used in this connection.   Though St Paul does not employ the actual word, his meaning in the later Epistles is identical, especially in Colossians.   In both places the unique Son of God, the Word by whom all things were made, was incarnate.   The Word of God existed before all things; they were created by him and for him, and thus the idea of inferior creators is eliminated.   For the Evangelist God is light and life, as in Psalm 119.   The thought that the Word of God is the light of the world is perfectly in harmony with Jewish thought.   Verse 11 of the Prologue might, indeed, be a very brief summary of the history of the Jewish people who, in the Old Testament, so constantly rejected God:

> He entered his own realm, and his own would not receive him.

In the following verse the 'faithful remnant', so prominent in Old Testament thought from the time of Isaiah, is brought to mind:

> To all who did receive him, to those who have yielded him their allegiance, he gave the right to become the children of God.

The Logos is that which is knowable of God: not only the thought behind the cosmos, but the creative power by which all things were made: God's power and thought in action.   This is the meaning given to it both by Philo and the Fourth Evangelist, and it has the 'dynamic' significance which 'word' always has in Hebrew thought.   In the Prologue we are given an account of Jesus as the Eternal

Word in relation to the world; in the remainder of the Fourth Gospel we are shown the 'Logos' in the Life of Jesus: the two aspects of the 'Word made Flesh'. Here there is a further point to be noticed. In the Old Testament the Word of God is an extension of the personality of Yahweh, but in the Prologue there is a new conception: the Logos stands over against God and is himself divine, which shows that within the riches of God's Being there are personal distinctions.[1]

In considering the Logos doctrine of St John's Prologue we must remember that it was formulated within the environment of the marvelling worship and wonder of the primitive Christian community. As every theologian is bound to do, the writer used the thought forms current in his time to give expression to the incomparable significance of Jesus, his Lord and God. Though St John was much more aware of Greek ways of thought than St Paul, he yet returns, behind these forms, to the deepest theology and messianic thinking of the Old Testament, seen in the light of Jesus Christ and his life-story. Thus his Gospel is radically Jewish and not Greek. In the Fourth Gospel salvation is still from the Jews:

It is from the Jews that salvation comes (4: 22).

Jesus is the true Temple:

but he was speaking of the temple of his body (2: 21).

The Old Testament, indeed, bears a vital part in this Gospel. Jesus is shown to be the crown of everything in Judaism:

[1] 'The distinctive feature of the Prologue is that the Logos stands over against God, and is himself divine, and this conception carries with it the view that within the riches of his Being there are personal distinctions.' (C. V. Taylor: *The Names of Jesus*, p. 164.)

it is as the King of the Jews that he goes to his death, and from the very first he is hailed as the 'King of Israel': 'Rabbi,' says Nathanael, 'you are the Son of God; you are the King of Israel.' St Peter says to him: 'Lord, to whom shall we go? Your words are words of eternal life. We have faith, and we know that you are the Holy One of God' (6: 69). He is the prophet like Moses who should come into the world:

> Surely this must be the prophet that was to come into the world (6: 14).

He is, above all, the Messiah, the Christ. Again and again the images Jesus is made to use of himself in this book—the Manna, the Light, the Shepherd, the Vine—all by their associations with the Old Testament and later Judaism show him to be in his own Person the true Israel of God. For this evangelist God is the Living God of the Prophets and Psalmists, not an abstract idea.[1] We may note, too, that St Paul confirms the fact that John's mission was to the Jews: 'James, Cephas and John, accepted Barnabas and myself as partners . . . agreeing that we should go to the Gentiles while they went to the Jews' (Gal. 2: 9).

Nevertheless, in spite of the work that has been expended upon it, the Fourth Gospel still remains an 'enigma'. Would we have it otherwise? Is it not fitting that this incomparable spiritual treasure, whose influence on the spiritual life of Christians has probably been greater than that of any of the other Gospels, should come to us as, in very truth, the 'Word of God', its origins wrapped in

[1] 'The sheer attractiveness of the life-story of Jesus formed the sharp spearpoint which pierced through the religiously empty heart of Hellenism, and opened the way for the Syrian doctrine of the "living God" to penetrate.' (G. Dix: *Jew and Greek*, p. 90.)

mystery? Yet there are rich gains from this modern study, and all the work expended on research on this Gospel has not proved unrewarding. Not the least of these gains is that it is now felt that a late date is quite impossible (Higgins, op. cit., p. 126). Though it may only have been completed about the turn of the century, its traditions are earlier still, and they are Palestinian. Secondly, whatever objections may still be raised against this view, it surely leaves us free, if we will, to accept the tradition of very great antiquity that it was written by the son of Zebedee himself. Or, failing this, that the memories of the 'beloved disciple' lie behind it. Burney suggested that our present Gospel was written by John the Elder, who was present at the Last Supper, and had a place next to Jesus. If we accept the authorship of St John, it would account for the acknowledged resemblance between this Gospel and that of St Mark. In both the figure of Jesus himself is dominant—that around which all revolves. Given the Petrine background of St Mark, this resemblance may easily be understood, and may well account for that sense of awe, of the 'numinous', which is produced by both books, for who better than those two, who had formed part of the most intimate circle of Jesus, could give us that impression —an impression that remains, as Dr Vincent Taylor has said, 'after years of brooding study'?[1]

As we cannot limit what God reveals to his saints in vision, much less can we judge what would be the outcome of the unique experience of St John, who in his youth lived in such close intimacy with the Incarnate Lord, who was with him at the Transfiguration and in Gethsemane, who leaned on his bosom at the Last Supper, and alone of his

[1] *The Person of Christ in New Testament Teaching*, p. 123.

disciples stood at the foot of the Cross.   Apart from this, what would he not have learned in those years in which he cared for the Mother of the Lord?

We must now return to our original question: how far can we see in this Gospel the Hellenisation of St Paul's message?   How far did the author write 'to show the historical Jesus preaching the mystical doctrine of redemption through being-in-the-logos-Christ'?   How far, again, was St Paul's 'en Christo' the background of the Johannine mysticism?

These are, of course, questions to which we can never, from their very nature, give a definite answer.   Yet the trend of modern study does lead us to agree with Professor Dodd that, though we may not exclude the possibility of Pauline influence from the Johannine mystical teaching, neither can we assume that the Johannine usage was dependent on the Pauline.[1]   Though the thought of St John is closely connected with that of St Paul, since both are great Christian mystics, yet it is not dependent upon it either in form or content.   In this connection it is interesting to consider the opinion of that very great Johannine scholar, Bishop Westcott.   Though he accepted apostolic authorship, he yet placed the actual writing of the Fourth Gospel somewhere about A.D. 100.   Among the reasons he gives for this comparatively late date is that this Gospel

> met difficulties which had not been and could not be felt till the preaching of St Paul had moulded the Christian Society in accordance with the law of freedom.   Then first the great problems as to *the nature of the object of personal faith*, as to the *revelation of the Deity*, as to the *universality* of the Gospel,

---

[1] *The Interpretation of the Fourth Gospel*, p. 193.

P.J.M.—F

were apprehended in their true vastness; and the Evangelist shows that these thoughts of a later age were not unregarded by Christ himself.[1]

Thus we can imagine readers of the Pauline letters, with their constantly reiterated phrase '$\dot{\epsilon}\nu$ $X\rho\iota\sigma\tau\hat{\omega}$ '$I\eta\sigma o\hat{\upsilon}$' asking, as we are asking today, what did St Paul really mean by it? To whom would they have turned but to the aged Apostle, who had seen and heard and handled the 'Word of Life'? If we accept this explanation, then we may see in the Fourth Gospel not a *dependence* on St Paul's '$\dot{\epsilon}\nu$ $X\rho\iota\sigma\tau\hat{\omega}$', but a clarifying, a deepening, a simplification of that which in the Pauline Epistles remains obscure. St Paul's Epistles, we will remember, were written under circumstances which left but little time for prolonged reflection, until those last Epistles which were written in Captivity. It is interesting to find how close the teaching of these Epistles of the Captivity does, in fact, come to that of St John.

[1] B. F. Westcott: *The Gospel of St John*, Introduction, p. xxxviii.

7

'Abide in me'

WHEREAS THE thought of St Paul is so complex and so many-sided that it is extremely difficult to analyse, since in it one concept is poured out in swift succession upon another, the thought of the Johannine writer presents difficulties which arise from the very opposite tendency. The thought here is so simple, and yet has such overtones of meaning, that it is no easy task to set it forth at all adequately. The writer goes over the same thoughts again and again, yet preserving perfect order and limpid clarity of expression, while the vocabulary is extremely limited. When considering this writer's contribution to the doctrine of life 'in Christ' there are, however, certain points which stand out very clearly.

In the first place, the use of 'ἐν Χριστῷ' is replaced by 'ἐν ἐμοί', 'in me'. The change is perfectly natural, for the phrase is placed upon the lips of Jesus himself. Most frequently the thought is carried further and brings us to the idea of union with God which, though implicit in the Pauline Epistles, is seldom expressed in them. Possibly St Paul, on account of his long grounding in the strictest Judaism, would hesitate to carry the thought of this intimate relationship so far. Traditionally the Jews of the later centuries before Christ refrained out of reverence from mentioning the divine name 'Yahweh'—with the result that much uncertainty exists as to how this word should actually be pronounced, and what vowels should be supplied for the consonants which alone figure in the Hebrew Bible. Secondly, the thought of St John is definitely 'locative'. This is made clear by his frequent use of the word 'abide', 'μένειν'. In fact, this word recurs so often both in the Gospel and the First Epistle of St John, which most scholars agree in attributing to the same writer, that it may possibly have been learnt from the Lord himself. It meets us in the very first chapter of the Gospel, where the two disciples of St John the Baptist (one of whom was surely the writer) come to Jesus and ask 'ποῦ μένεις'; 'where dwellest thou?', or 'where abidest thou?': words which give us the keynote to all his later teaching. This is the question St John sets himself to answer: 'Where abidest thou?': who are you, where do you live, what is the mystery surrounding you? Jesus answers very simply, 'come and see.'

May we not see behind this familiar story the questionings that were being raised about Jesus, the crucified and risen Lord, whom his followers proclaimed with such radiant zeal and devotion? There it was, so simple, so arresting, so transfiguring. The story was in all probability told at first to the simplest men and women as they gathered by the wayside or in some country inn, and always it told of One who had been crucified, who died and was buried, and yet who rose from the dead and was alive for evermore. Strange miracles, too, were performed by his followers, so that the people ran after them, crowded upon them, as they had upon their Master in his lifetime. Peter and John cure a cripple by the 'Beautiful Gate' of the Temple, and people run up in amazement to see what has taken place, whereupon Peter disowns all credit for this cure, and declares that 'the name of Jesus, by awakening faith, has strengthened this man, whom ye see and know, and this faith has made him completely well, as you can see for yourselves' (Acts 3: 16). The sick were carried out into the streets 'and laid there on beds and stretchers so that even the shadow of Peter might fall on one or another of them as he passed by' (Acts 5: 15). What questions this must have raised in the minds of the people, and as the Gospel was carried to the Gentile world by St Paul and his companions fresh questions would have been raised, different minds would have grappled with these strange accounts of One who had been put to death and who had risen again, and was declared to be the Son of God with power. Since Jesus died for all, the faith must be set forth in a way that all could understand. Here, in the very first chapter, the pattern is set before us. The two disciples went and dwelt with Jesus that day, and then proclaimed to their friends that they had found the Messias, the Christ. Nathanael hails him as the 'Son of God', the 'King of Israel', and Jesus, accepting this, in his answer uses the name he best loved for himself:

> In truth, in very truth I tell you, that you shall see the heaven wide open, and God's angels ascending and descending upon the Son of Man.

Here the central thoughts of St John's teaching are brought together in great simplicity, but with far-reaching associations, which we cannot now stop to consider. The Evangelist wrote his Gospel to give his answer to this immense mystery; the answer he had gathered from 'abiding' long with Jesus.

The Fourth Gospel converges absolutely upon the Person of Jesus himself, and it is this convergence that makes it so difficult to analyse. There are such subtle shades and distinctions, such rich and wide implications, that its treasures are as inexhaustible as are those of the Pauline writings. How could it be otherwise, since these pages seek in such small compass to set before us not only the life story of the incarnate Lord, but also the doctrines of his Nature and Being? Here we can but touch very briefly on certain aspects stressed by the writer in his portrayal of Jesus—points which bear directly on our theme. For the Evangelist it is the *Life* of Jesus which is of supreme importance, and, though he is no less Christocentric than St Paul, his emphasis is rather upon the divine-human quality of Christ's life on earth than on Christ the heavenly and regnant Lord. The thought that Jesus is 'the same yesterday, today and for ever' is yet never far from the surface of his thoughts: he never loses sight of the fact that Jesus is the Eternal Son of God. In him, and in him alone, he sees all the meaning of this world and of the life of men.

One of the first elements in his portrayal of the 'Holy One of God' is that which a recent writer has seen to be the essential characteristic of the concept of holiness: his perfect vision.

> He knew men so well, all of them, that he needed no evidence from others about a man, for he himself could tell what was in a man (John 2: 25).

His words to Nathanael: 'Here is an Israelite worthy of the name; there is nothing false in him' brings the surprised question, 'How do you know me?' Jesus replies, 'I saw you under the fig tree before Philip spoke to you', and this evokes the immediate response of marvelling faith:

> Rabbi, you are the Son of God, you are the King of Israel (1: 47–49).

The Samaritan woman, after speaking with him as he sat by the well, went to tell her friends that she had found one who had told her all she had done:

> Come and see a man who has told me everything I ever did. Could this be the Messiah? (4 : 29).

Many Samaritans believed on him because of the woman's saying, but many more because they heard it from his own lips and said to the woman:

> It is no longer because of what you said that we believe, for we have heard him ourselves; and we know that this is the Saviour of the world (4 : 42).

He with whom the disciples abode in such close intimacy left them with the impression that he knew all things without being told, that he could look into the deep recesses of men's hearts and read their inmost thoughts. To abide 'in him', therefore, means being with One who, without being told, without even asking of us the effort of self-disclosure, knows our deepest need and can supply all we ask. Indeed, he knows what we really long for, though we ourselves do not know that we long for it; he knows what we most deeply desire, while we only feel a strange hunger and need which of ourselves we cannot explain. To awaken that need in men's hearts, in their *conscious* lives, bringing it up out of the depth of the unconscious, and thus to be able to satisfy that need, was the mission of the Son of God.

Another point that arises in these earlier chapters is the quiet assurance with which difficult and dangerous situations are met. The quite ordinary predicament of the ruler at the wedding feast in Cana when the wine threatened to run short was solved in so masterly a fashion, with so little display, that it brought conviction. This was the first

'sign' that Jesus did, 'and his disciples believed on him'
(2: 11). We find it again in chapter 6, not only in the
miraculous feeding of the hungry multitudes, but also when
his disciples, caught in a sudden storm at night as they were
in the middle of the sea, struggling to bring their boat to
shore in safety, saw him coming to them on the waters.
Quite naturally they were filled with fear—terrified—but
he called out to them, 'It is I; do not be afraid.' Then
'they were ready to take him aboard, and immediately the
boat reached the land they were making for' (6: 19, 20).
The Synoptists record this happening in various ways, and
it is perfectly well authenticated, but this conclusion is
given by St John alone: 'immediately they were at the land
whither they went' (A.V.). St Paul had said this very
differently:

> the whole universe was created through him and for him!
> And he exists before everything, and all things are held
> together by him (Col. 1: 16, 17).

The underlying thought is identical; its expression could
scarcely be more different. It is the fundamental truth
that impressed itself upon the Apostolic band: in him, in
Christ, is the full and true meaning of all life and being: to
be 'in him' is to find our true end; for him to be 'in us',
or to come to us, fulfils all our need. He is the *end* of the
way, as he is the beginning. The great Christian Apocalypse speaks of him as 'Alpha and Omega', the first and the
last, the beginning and the end' (Rev. 22: 13).

In the third chapter the Bride and Bridegroom motif
which we have also found in St Paul is very briefly mentioned in words attributed to St John the Baptist:

> It is the bridegroom to whom the bride belongs. The
> bridegroom's friend, who stands by and listens to him, is

overjoyed at hearing the bridegroom's voice. This joy, this perfect joy, is now mine. As he grows greater, I must grow less (3 : 29).

It is followed by a passage characteristic of this Evangelist:

He whom God sent utters the words of God, so measureless is God's gift of the Spirit. The Father loves the Son and has entrusted him with all authority. He who puts his faith in the Son has hold of eternal life (3 : 34–63).

This is echoed again in chapter 5 :

The Son can do nothing of himself; he does only what he sees his Father doing; what the Father does the Son does. For the Father loves the Son and shows him all his works, and will show greater yet, to fill you with wonder. As the Father raises the dead and gives them life, so the Son gives life to men (5 : 19).

To have union with the Son, to be 'in Christ', is to have eternal life. To have union with the Son is also to have union with the Father.

In truth, in very truth I tell you, the believer possesses eternal life (6 : 47).

This is eternal life : to know thee who alone art truly God, and Jesus Christ whom thou hast sent (17 : 3).

This, then, is the ultimate meaning of life 'in Christ': it is to have everlasting life through the knowledge of God in Christ.

In the tenth chapter comes the tremendous statement:

My Father and I are one (10 : 30).

Quite clearly and definitely to be *in* Christ is to be *in* the Father, since they are one.

You study the scriptures diligently [says Jesus to the Jews], supposing that in them you have eternal life; yet, although their testimony points to me, you refuse to come to me for that life (5 : 39).

It is the Father's will that everyone who looks to the Son and has faith in him shall possess eternal life—'And I will raise him up at the last day' (6: 40). The yearning, humble love of the God of the Old Testament shows through in these chapters: 'Him that cometh to me I will in no wise case out' (6: 37).

*   *   *

St Thomas Aquinas once wrote: 'Holy Scripture is called the Heart of Christ because it reveals his heart.' Nowhere is this heart of love so perfectly shown to us as it is in the closing chapters of the Fourth Gospel, both in the great Last Discourses and in the picture St John gives of the Lord in the last hours of his earthly life.

Judas had gone out into the night to betray his Master, and Jesus gives his last message to his faithful band of disciples:

> My children . . . where I am going you cannot come. I give you a new commandment: love one another; as I have loved you, so you are to love one another. If there is love among you, then all will know that you are my disciples (13: 33–35).

This is the one thing needful. Whereas the other New Testament writers give us various moral precepts, in St John all is gathered up into the one simple command to love. This is surely a sign of one who had lived long in realised union with God—God who *is* love. In the First Epistle, which was probably written some years later and intended for the same circle of believers as the Gospel, he enlarges upon this precept of love, and shows the importance of its place in human life. He must then have been of a great age, and his spiritual vision had become extremely simple and clear.   Possibly those early Christians had been asking how they could know that they possessed this love, which was the one thing needful.   The answer, given in the simplest language, insists upon the necessity of 'abiding in him'.

As he taught you, then, abide in him (1 John 2: 27).

And if they thus dwell in him, they dwell also in the Father, and this brings with it the promise of eternal life.

By this we know what love is: that Christ laid down his life for us (3: 16).

Love must show itself in action, in brotherly love.   God's command is that we believe in his Son and love one another, and

When we keep his commandments we dwell in him and he in us (3: 24).

Let us love one another, because love is from God.   Everyone who loves is a child of God and knows God, but the unloving know nothing of God.   For God is love; and his love is disclosed to us in this, that he sent his only-begotten Son into the world to bring us life.   The love I speak of is not our love for God, but the love he showed to us in sending his Son as the remedy for the defilement of our sins . . . Though God has never been seen by any man, God dwells in us if we love one another; his love is brought to perfection in us. (4: 7–12).

The Johannine conception of eternal life is wholly in accordance with the old prophetic concern for the 'here and now', and the Old Testament insistence on the primacy of faith and trust in God.   In the Old Testament, faith in resurrection rests ultimately on the conviction of the righteousness of God: his justice, power and graciousness. If men live in his faith and love and suffer for him, surely, since he is a righteous God, just and merciful, he will vindicate them. The resurrection of Jesus confirmed and manifested God's victory over death and evil. In the Last Discourses, written of necessity in the light of the resurrection, Jesus gives his disciples an assurance which, though it has a note of eschatology, is yet in line with the old, sober teaching of the Old Testament.

> Trust in God always; trust also in me. There are many dwelling-places in my Father's house; if it were not so I would have told you; for I am going there on purpose to prepare a place for you . . . that where I am there you may be also (14: 1–3).

In the thought of St Paul, Christ and the ethical and temporal considerations are central to his eschatology. The Christian, since he belongs to Christ, is 'in Christ Jesus', partakes already of life which is true life. In St John, too, the union between God and the believer is the fulfilment of eternal life: he has no purely apocalyptic interpretation of eternal life, for this can begin here and now, in union with Christ. Life in Heaven is the fulfilment of that life which begins already in this world.

Many of Christ's words in the Fourth Gospel refer to mysteries which could only be understood in the future, and this applies especially to the Last Discourses. In fact, we may say that only after Christ's death and resurrection, when they partook of the Sacraments, would his followers understand what at the time must have seemed extremely puzzling to them. While this Gospel is the most speculative of all the Gospels, it is also the most concrete. Christ is shown as a spirituality quite beyond our reach, and yet he is perfectly human.   Moreover, here the most historical acts of the Lord's life are blended with St. John's teaching concerning our union with Christ.   Between the events of his life and the doctrine of our union with him there is no break, and it is St John's concern to see that there is no break.   Yet, while he stresses the importance of the life of Jesus, he is nevertheless the most heavenly of all the Evangelists.   He sees the *life* of Jesus to be of such vital importance because in it we see God: to know Jesus is to know the Father, for they are one.

> If I go and prepare a place for you [says Jesus] I shall come again and receive you to myself so that where I am you may be also; and my way there is known to you (14: 3).

Thomas said: 'Lord, we do not know where you are going, so how can we know the way?' and Jesus answers:

> I am the way; I am the truth and I am the life; no man cometh to the Father except by me (14: 4–6).
> Lord, show us the Father and we ask no more [asks Philip]. (14: 8).

This was, actually, a perfectly legitimate question: it was right that they should desire to see God, the Father, yet it showed that Philip had failed to realise, after years spent with his Master, that his prayer had been answered; that to live with Jesus was to have the vision of God:

> Have I been so long time with you, Philip, and still you do not know me?   Anyone who has seen me has seen the Father . . . Believe me when I say that I am in the Father and the Father in me; or else accept the evidence of the deeds themselves (14: 9 ff.).

> If you ask anything in my name I will do it, that the Father may be glorified in the Son (v. 13).

The Father abides in the Son and the Son in the Father.
The Church has given to this divine union the name 'cir-
cumincession'. Our indwelling in Christ is to be understood in a sense that resembles, however imperfectly, this
mutual indwelling of the Divine Persons: it is a perfect
inwardness, bearing a remote resemblance to the life of
love of the Blessed Trinity.

> Anyone who loves me will heed what I say; then my Father
> will love him, and we will come to him and make our
> dwelling with him . . . I have told you while I am still here
> with you; but your Advocate, the Holy Spirit whom the
> Father will send in my name, will teach you everything,
> and will call to mind all that I have told you. (14: 23 ff.).

St Paul spoke of the fruits of the Spirit (Gal. 5: 22)—
love, joy, peace; St John shows us the source of these
'fruits' to be in the Heart of Jesus himself. In union with
him, and in no other way, can these fruits of the Spirit
manifest themselves in our lives.

Jesus compares himself to the vine:

> I am the vine, you are the branches. He who dwells in me,
> as I dwell in him, bears much fruit; for apart from me ye
> can do nothing. He who does not dwell in me is thrown
> away like a withered branch (15: 5, 6).

On this last night he says: 'Peace is my parting gift to you,
my own peace, such as the world cannot give' (14: 27).
And again: 'For the moment you are sad at heart; but I
shall see you again, and then you will be joyful, and no one
shall rob you of your joy' (16: 22).

For St John the union of the Father and the Son is so
close that to see the Son—the Incarnate Word—is in actual
fact to see the Father also. In fact, he knows no other
'vision of God' but that which is given us in the divine self-

revelation in Jesus Christ. The eternal and incomprehensible God must always remain withdrawn from our sight and is beyond our grasp except in so far as we see him in Christ. Yet the union of the Father and the Son and the Holy Spirit—the Blessed and Holy Trinity—is so perfect that to see and know the One is to see and know the Three. That which the Father wills the Son wills, and the Holy Spirit is the perfect bond of union between them. Between the will of the Father and that of the Son and that of the Holy Spirit there is no hiatus; they will one will, and yet the distinctions of Person remain within the Godhead. What the Son does is in reality the activity of the Father:

> My Father has never ceased his work, and I am working too (5: 17).

> The Son can do nothing of himself; he does only what he sees the Father doing; what the Father does the Son does (5: 19).

The Son does the Father's works and speaks his words:

> I do nothing on my own authority, but in all that I say, I have been taught by my Father (8: 28).

The Gospel of St John has been described as the 'gospel of pure relationship'[1] for the relationship between the Father and the Son is here shown to be the archetype of that between Christ and his disciples, and ideally, that amongst the disciples themselves, one with another:

> As thou, Father, art in me, and I in thee, so also may they be one in us, that the world may believe that thou didst send me. The glory which thou gavest me I have given to them, that they may be one, as we are one; I in them and thou in me, may they be perfectly one (17: 22, 23).

[1] M. Buber: *I and Thou*, p. 85.

This relationship between the Father and the Son is a *dynamic*, not a static one; it is the sharing of one divine life and activity rooted in the love of God.

That access to the Father is by Christ alone we have also seen to be the innermost kernel of the Pauline Epistles. The Fourth Evangelist inherits the whole wealth of primitive traditional language, but his contribution to the development of Christian theology is to have simplified it by discarding what was purely Jewish and causing all the rest to converge upon Christ alone. The situation in which he wrote was no longer that of St Paul, whose struggles with the Jewish Christians were a thing of the past; they had broken down in A.D. 70. For St John the struggle is rather that between darkness and light, between good and evil—a struggle that is found expressed even in the most primitive forms of religion—and must, in fact, always remain an element in all religious thought, since it is part of that world in which man finds himself, and from which he cannot escape. St John is no longer concerned with questions of the Law, but with a much wider and more universal concept.

At the moment Christ accepts death (and glorification) Satan is cast out, his dominion is ended: 'the Prince of this world stands condemned' (16 : 11). Christ's last words to his disciples before he goes to meet his death are words of encouragement and triumph:

But courage! The victory is mine; I have conquered the world (16: 33).

Here it may be well to pause for a moment to consider what this actually implies. Though we may not deny the value of the scholastic conception of the Redemption

wrought by Christ as a reparation for man's sin—the
juridical aspect—yet this view of the Atonement is far from
exhausting its meaning. As a consequence of the Fall
man was cast out of Eden: out of the place into which God
had brought him in order to keep him under his own
protection, safe from the attacks of evil spirits. In the
garden—in Paradise—man could only know God through
the interior life, in his inmost soul, responding quite simply
to the divine inspirations. When, after the Fall, man was
cast out of the garden, though it is true that he was still
under the divine protection, and that God in his love prepared for him skins to clothe himself with, yet he became
subject to the temptations and insinuations of the fallen
angels: he became a sharer in their revolt against their
Creator. Distracted by the sights and sounds of this world,
he no longer heard the still, small voice of God speaking
within, and thus fell under the dominion of Satan. According to St Thomas Aquinas, the Devil belonged to that
order of angels to whom dominion was given over the things
of this world. Even material things are dominated by
spirits, and, as Teilhard de Chardin said somewhere, everything has an 'inner' life. Therefore, when cast out of
Paradise, out of the special sphere of God's protecting grace,
man naturally fell under the sway of this fallen order of
angels.

When we are brought into union with God in Christ we
are thereby set free from the power and dominion of Satan,
the 'Prince of this world'. The redemption in Christ in
which we participate is not only something that takes place
between us and God, it is a drama which affects the whole
creation—a drama in which man shares. To understand
the faith of St Paul we must take into account this 'cosmic'

aspect of redemption, and this applies with equal force to
the Johannine teaching.   One of the consequences of the
Fall was death.   Therefore, in order to deliver man from
all the consequences of his separation from God—from the
power of the Devil and from death—Jesus must vanquish
death by undergoing it himself.   Man still dies, but the
sting is taken out of death because the Christian is 'in
Christ': he is a sharer in the great victory over evil.   This
may help to throw some light on that word which we have
seen recurs so frequently in the Johannine writings—'μένειν'
'abide'.   To 'abide' in Christ is, in some sense, a return
to Paradise.   One spiritual state excludes another: to abide
in union with the Sacred Heart of Jesus is to be brought out
of the sphere of Satan's dominion.   The 'Lamb of God'
takes away the sins of the world by uniting us with himself.

8

'τετέλεσται'—'It is finished'

THE SYNOPTISTS show us Jesus constantly winning the victory over the powers of evil in the days of his active ministry: they tell of the victory over the temptations of the Devil in the wilderness, of repeated cures, casting out evil spirits, healing the sick. All these were part of the great struggle against the enemy. St Paul, however, makes no mention of these lesser victories over evil, for the victory Christ won on the Cross was for him so utterly supreme that he did not pause to speak of the earlier ones. This can only be partially true of St John, because, although he, too, concentrated upon the victory of the Cross, we must, I think, believe that he knew the three earlier Gospels, and there was, consequently, no need for him to repeat what had already been so adequately portrayed in them. He concentrates, rather, upon showing Jesus as meeting the very deepest needs of mankind in their desire for union with God. He shows us that the events in the life of Jesus embody the eternal ideas they represent most perfectly. Bread, light, vine and water are not mere illustrations:

the symbol is absorbed into the reality it signifies.[1]

Jesus is the *true* light: 'I am the light of the world'; the

[1] C. H. Dodd: *The Interpretation of the Fourth Gospel*, p. 140.

true light that lightens every man coming into the world. This is the light that flamed in the Burning Bush, the light that the lamps of the Feast of Hanukkah symbolised, for there was no richer symbol of the sovereignty of God and his appointed kings than the 'lamp of Israel' (cp. 2 Sam. 1: 17; 1 Kings 2: 36; 15: 4, etc.). For the Fourth Evangelist the thought of light shining in the darkness and never quenched by it is of great importance. Chapter 9 is the classical instance of Jesus giving sight or light to a man born blind:

> It is for judgment that I am come into the world—to give sight to the sightless and to make blind those who see (9: 39).

The only *true* Food is that which the Son of Man gives, for Jesus has life in himself, and can give it abundantly to all his brethren:

> I am the Bread of Life (6: 35).

Manna, the bread from heaven, was always regarded in Jewish apocalyptic as one of the blessings of the Messianic age, and in Philo as a symbol of the Logos. The Jews say to Jesus:

> Our ancestors had manna to eat in the desert; as Scripture says, He gave them bread from heaven (6: 31).

Jesus answers:

> The truth is not that Moses gave you the bread from heaven, but that my Father gives you the real bread from heaven. The bread that God gives comes down from heaven and brings life to the world (6: 32, 33).

The feeding of the multitude with loaves nurtures their souls with eternal life, for Christ, who gives them the

Bread *is* the Bread of Life. As food becomes interior to those who eat, so Christ will become interior to those who feed on him: he will dwell in them, and they in him.

The symbolism of the Vine is equally clear. The 'Vine' in St John takes the place of the 'Body' in St Paul. Through the prophet Isaiah, God had spoken of Israel as the vineyard:

> The vineyard of the Lord of hosts is the house of Israel (Is. 5: 7).

The psalmist spoke of her as the vine:

> Thou hast brought a vine out of Egypt . . . and planted it (Ps. 80: 8).

> I am the real Vine [says Jesus] and my Father is the gardener . . . Dwell in me, as I in you. No branch can bear fruit of itself, but only if it remains united with the vine; no more can ye bear fruit, unless you remain united with me (15: 1–4).

The first is but a shadow of the reality; now a mystical identification has taken place. In his beloved Son, God says, 'I am the true Vine.' The first Vine represented the people; some of its branches are dead, some produce fruit. They are *part* of the Vine, but the *whole* vine is Christ himself. Any fruits that the branches produce are rooted in Christ, they flow from him, who is the root of the Vine. Through him his children are brought into that divine life which flows from the Father to the Son. Those who abide in him in faith and love will know him, for he has promised to manifest himself to them and to be with them:

> Anyone who loves me will heed what I say; then my Father will love him, and we will come to him, and make our dwelling with him (14: 23).

A man who receives my commands and obeys them—he it is who loves me; and he who loves me will be loved of my Father; and I will love him and disclose myself to him (14: 21).

Water in the Fourth Gospel, though in a few places it has the simple and obvious connotation of cleansing, usually contains in it some of the rich and varied symbolism which water held for the ancient world, both in Jewish thought and in that of the surrounding cultures.

In place of the many miracles of the synoptic gospels St John shows us the 'signs' of Jesus. Now the sign does not of necessity denote anything miraculous. It is a term applied especially to the symbolic acts performed by the prophets of the Old Testament. They were inspired to see in such symbolic acts the will and power of God. Allowing themselves to be used by him, as channels of his grace, their mighty 'signs' formed the prelude to that which God had determined to perform in history. The 'signs' of St John come very near to this view, but they refer, in the first instance, 'to timeless realities signified by the act in time.'[1] Yet this was not their whole import, for

> Christ's work of giving light and life is accomplished in reality and actuality by the historical act of his Death and Resurrection. In that sense every 'sign' in the narrative points forward to the great climax.[2]

The raising of Lazarus thus foreshadowed his own death and resurrection by which God would be supremely glorified: 'I am the resurrection and the life.' There is no way to *true* life but through union with Jesus—a union consummated in his Passion and death.

[1] Dodd, op cit.
[2] ibid., p. 142.

For St John all the things and events in the life of Jesus are

> a living and moving image of the eternal, and not a veil of illusion to hide it.[1]

Jesus, in his own Person, sums up what the Kingdom of God means, for

> The Kingdom of Heaven is Christ Jesus exhorting all men to repentance, and *drawing them to himself by grace.*[2]

In the great High-priestly prayer in chapter 17 the whole thought revolves around the union of men with God and with one another. Till then the Fourth Gospel had been concerned with the individual Christian's union with Christ—the thought that each Christian is *in* Christ and Christ *in* him—but here it widens out to embrace all mankind. Christ prays that we may all be one, even as he and the Father are one (v. 11) and

> As thou, Father, art in me, and I in thee, may they also be one in us (17: 21).

This is the climax of the whole Gospel. The Incarnate Lord includes all believers in himself and brings them into union with the Father.

We must now turn to the supreme 'sign', to which all the signs in this Gospel are but the prelude: the Death of Christ upon the Cross. The thought that Christ is glorified and exalted in his Death must be understood in an absolute sense in the Gospel, for here is revealed most perfectly the love of God—his divine 'agape'. This is the glory that Christ had with the Father from the beginning,

---

[1] ibid., p. 143.
[2] Origen: in Matt. 11: 15.

before the foundation of the world, and this therefore
brings us the thought that the Crucifixion is actually an
event on the spiritual plane.   To this the Resurrection can
add nothing:

> In dying Christ is going to the Father, and this is to live in
> the fullest possible sense of the word (C. H. Dodd: op. cit.,
> p. 441).

In this connection it is interesting to note that Bishop
Westcott drew attention to the fact that in his First Epistle
St John makes no mention of the Resurrection, and that
Professor Mersch considers that in his teaching on the
Mystical Body of Christ St Paul had not fully worked out the
implications of the Resurrection.

> I have glorified thee on earth by *completing* the work thou
> gavest me to do (17: 4).

Here Christ declares the work to be completed, perfected,
on the spiritual plane, but it is only completed as a concrete
act in history when the sacrifice is consummated on the
Cross:

> Jesus, aware that all had now come *to its appointed end*, said,
> in fulfilment of Scripture, 'I thirst' (19: 28).

In both places the same Greek word is used, and it is sus-
ceptible of many shades of meaning.   Under the different
aspects of this word and that which it implies we may
think that prophecy, and the earthly work of Christ and,
in fact, Christ himself, were 'made perfect'.   Every essential element in the portraiture of the Messiah had been
fulfilled; the 'end' of all had been attained.   Nothing was
left undone.

> He said 'τετέλεσται'—'it is finished' (19: 30).

Traditionally, almost without exception, this Greek word has been rendered in English translations 'It is finished'. Knox gives 'It is achieved'; the N.E.B. 'It is accomplished'. Luther has 'es ist vollbracht'—achieved, accomplished. A modern Russian translation (1955) uses an expression denoting achievement of a high aim—like reaching the top of Mount Everest, or getting to the moon. Since the Greek root 'τελ' allows of a great variety of connotation, we cannot readily come to a conclusion as to the exact meaning of the great cry from the Cross. Possibly 'My purpose is accomplished' comes as near as anything else to its real meaning, denoting not only termination, but also purpose, which are the two dominant ideas conveyed by the Greek. 'It is finished' contains in itself these two shades of meaning: *finishing* an appointed task, *perfecting* something, and thus making it ready for use. We say a house is 'finished' when we mean that it is ready to be lived in, thus implying both termination and purpose.

Westcott pointed out that here the absence of a definite subject forces the reader to call to mind each work that is here brought to an end. Here all the great types of the Old Testament are fulfilled: Jesus is the Paschal Lamb; as Moses lifted up the brazen serpent in the wilderness that those who looked upon it might be saved so the Son of Man is lifted up to draw all men to himself:

I, if I be lifted up from the earth, will draw all men to myself (12:32).

Surely there is significance in this Death on the Cross, for only thus could Jesus be 'lifted up', as he could not have been had he been slain by the sword as was James, or suffered the Jewish 'stoning' like Stephen, or died by 'burning' like Nero's victims. May we not see in the fact that Jesus lived and died at a time when Palestine was under Roman rule, and that he therefore endured the normal Roman punishment, the working of that mysterious Divine Providence, that perfect timing, that interplay of cause and event, which formed so great a part of the Hebrew faith and outlook? Just at that time, in that place, crucifixion happened to be the penalty meted out to a criminal under the power that ruled.

Again, Jesus is the 'Good Shepherd' of the psalmist:

> I am the good shepherd; I know my own sheep and my sheep know me—as the Father knows me and I know the Father—and I lay down my life for the sheep (10: 14, 15).

He is the door by which alone the sheep may enter the fold and find pasture. He is the grain of wheat falling into the ground to die that we may live.

Furthermore, it is not only the types and prophecies of the Old Testament that are completed and fulfilled in him, but also those concepts which had developed so slowly in the history of God's Chosen People. There is, for instance, that mysterious concept of the 'holy', a subject most obscure, and regarding which diverse views have been held by scholars. Rudolf Otto, in his *Idea of the Holy*, says:

> It remains inexpressible and ineffable . . . and completely eludes comprehension in terms of concepts. The God of the New Testament is not less holy than the God of the Old Testament, but more holy . . . the unworthiness of the profane in contact with him is not diminished, but made absolute . . . 'The Word', 'the Spirit', 'the Person of Jesus', becomes that to which man flees, in which he finds refuge and in which he 'locks himself', in order that conse-

crated and cleansed of his 'profaneness' thereby he may come
into the presence of holiness itself.[1]

By his victory of love Christ has prepared a place for us
into which we may, nay, we *must* enter, if we would find
union with God: that place himself. 'Abide in me.' The
Old Testament concept of God was not so much that of
vision, but of God as the rock: 'El Shaddai'. This was
probably the idea that formed itself in the mind of Abraham
at the time of his call, and which sustained him in com-
mitting himself to the unknown way: 'God omnipotent'
—able to protect him in all places.

> I will love thee, O Lord my strength [cries the psalmist],
> the Lord is my stony rock and my defence: my Saviour, my
> God, and my might, in whom I will trust, my buckler, the
> horn also of my salvation, and my refuge (Ps. 18: 1).

Not till the Incarnate Lord had endured, in extremity of
pain, all that the malice and wickedness of man could
inflict upon him; not till he had suffered all the assaults of
'principalities and powers', of the 'rulers of the darkness
of this world' of spiritual wickedness in high places (Eph.
6: 10), not till then could he say 'It is finished'—perfected,
bombproof—that shelter of Love he had prepared for his
children. Only death can set the seal to a life. Perpetu-
ally he draws the souls of men into union with himself—
'Jesus Christ, the same yesterday, today and for ever'.
That union, beginning here and now, is destined to be our
ever-deepening joy and wonder through all the ages of
eternity.

'Finished', 'perfected', here is the revelation of the
Heart of Christ—the Heart of God. We have seen that

[1] op. cit., p. 58.

in the Johannine Discourses, written in the light of the
Resurrection, the Heart of the Incarnate Lord is shown
forth.   Here is the perfect fulfilment of the nuptial relationship with God proclaimed by the prophets, but also
apparent in the myth and ritual—the sacred marriage rites
—of the Ancient Near East cultures.   Here at last, clearly
shown forth, that which the mystics of all ages have dimly
discerned, and for which the heart of man so deeply longs:
love, assurance, compassion and holiness, revealed as infinite and boundless, since that human Person in whom they
are found is declared to be the Eternal Son of God, by
whom all things were made.

St John shows us Paradise in the Heart of Jesus.

When St Paul spoke of those things which God has prepared for them that love him, things surpassing all our
imaginings, surely he was thinking of the ever-growing and
deepening knowledge of Christ, and in him of the Blessed
Trinity, which God has prepared for us from the foundation
of the world, and before which all the paradise myths and
concepts of the Old Testament fall into insignificance.
Here St John is strangely 'modern', for one of the marks of
modern thought is its concentration on the 'person', on
'personality'.

> One of the soldiers stabbed his side with a lance, and at once
> there was a flow of blood and water (30: 34).

Jesus gives the 'living water' that flows from under the
Temple in the great vision of Ezekiel (ch. 47), and since
the water flows from his side he is both King and Temple.
The Fathers interpreted the meaning of the double stream
in different ways.   St Augustine sees here the opening
wide 'the door of life, from which the sacraments of the

Church have flowed out, without which there is no entering into true life', but he has a further thought:

> Noah was bidden to make a door in the side of the Ark, by which should enter thereunto the living creatures that should not perish in the Flood by which figures the Church was prefigured.

This double thought is of great value, and has had an incalculable influence on the devotional life of Christians. It is the thought which, developing very slowly, has at last blossomed into the devotion to the Sacred Heart of Jesus, which is now so widespread.[1]

St John, in the last chapters of his Gospel, shows us what was the nature of this Heart of Jesus, the human heart of the Son of God, for we dare not leave out the human character of Jesus and concentrate only upon the glorified Christ, since in so doing we shall fail to 'see Jesus' and thus to 'know God'. He shows us Jesus weeping at the graveside of his friend before raising him to life; on the last night of his life 'having loved his own which were in the world', he took a towel and girded himself, and then performed an act of exquisite humility by washing the feet of his disciples—an act that has imprinted itself very deeply on the mind of the Church and in her liturgy. We may think of the significance of this 'feet-washing' in many ways, but there is a beautiful suggestion made somewhere, I think, by Dr Leslie Weatherhead, that this 'feet-washing' was the initial ceremony at a Jewish wedding feast, and thus Jesus performs this ceremony as the initial act of his

[1] Though St John Eudes was apparently the first to seek to formulate a devotion to the Sacred Heart—a devotion which the Holy See, after much deliberation, finally sanctioned in the form promulgated by St Margaret Mary—it seems to me that we must see this devotion in germ in this passage of St Augustine.

death upon the Cross whereby he consummated his marriage with humanity. On that last night he bequeathed to them his joy and his peace, and promised that whatsoever they asked in his name he would give them, that the Father might be glorified. When apprehended in the garden on that fateful night Jesus offered himself up at once for capture that those who were with him might go free, and that none of those the Father had given him might be lost (Jn. 18: 8, 9). Then, hanging on the Cross in extremity of pain his thought still goes out to others, to his mother and the beloved disciple, whose grief he knew to be so intense, and he gives them to each other for their mutual consolation (19: 26, 27).

The task 'finished', 'accomplished', by Jesus on the Cross, the 'place prepared', the 'unspeakable gift of God' (2 Cor. 9: 15) was the whole Person and character of the Incarnate Lord, perfected there on the Cross. Deserted, outcast, crucified, he never ceased for a single moment to be himself: the beloved Lord who had convinced his followers that he was the Alpha and Omega, the first and the last, by whom all things were made, and to whom all things move as to their appointed end. Jesus is the centre of all history, which is first but a preparation for his coming, and then an entering, slowly and falteringly, into all that he has revealed to us. There is no cry of anguish here, but absolute mastery—'No man taketh my life from me, I lay it down of myself'—serenity, compassion. It is noteworthy that St John, who insists most passionately both in his Gospel and in the First Epistle on the unique value and importance of the *humanity* of Jesus Christ, also shows us his divine *impassibility*. Or shall we say, rather, his perfected humanity. The balance is perfect. It is this perfect balance, expressed with such mature simplicity, and possibly never again attained by any writer, that brings me the conviction that this Fourth Gospel must be the work of him who leaned on the Lord's bosom at the Last Supper, and learned divine secrets, and who, after a long life lived in realised union with his Lord and Master, wrote down his memories—memories inspired, surely, by the divine Lord himself.

9

Baptism into Union with Christ 'in his Death'

BOTH IN the Pauline and the Johannine teaching 'being-in-Christ' or union with Christ, is brought about, at least in the normal way, by the Sacraments—the 'post-resurrection miracles' (Cullmann). Insight into the meaning of the Sacraments—and of much else in the Paschal Mystery—could only come after the death and glorification of Jesus, when his Spirit was released into his followers. The promise of a coming perfect knowledge could not be understood until it was realised that it referred to insight into the mystery of the sacraments. Dr Schweitzer held that wherever the Spirit was promised, there the sacraments are to be understood; and where the sacraments are spoken of, there the coming of the Holy Spirit is implied in the Fourth Gospel, since

> The Spirit is nothing else than the Logos, no longer limited to his historical manifestation in Jesus Christ. Jesus describes the coming of the Spirit as being also his own personal coming again to his own.[1]

Only when Jesus is again with them as the Spirit can their 'being-in-him' begin. So long as he is with them in the flesh they can listen to his discourses, but they cannot be 'in him'. Therefore, it is only after the Death of Jesus

[1] op. cit., p. 353.

that there can be a 'being-in-Christ'.   In this respect the Pauline and Johannine mysticism are entirely at one.

Actually, however, this is a point which has given rise to no little discussion, for neither St Paul nor St John is perfectly consistent on this point: in some places they insist that baptism is the entry into 'life in Christ', whereas in others this is brought about by faith.   For instance, in the third chapter of St John's Gospel, Jesus says:

> unless a man has been born again he cannot see the kingdom of God . . . no one can enter the kingdom of God without being born of water and the spirit (3 : 5),

and baptism is made the prerequisite for entry into blessedness, whereas a few verses further on in the same chapter he says:

> This Son of man must be lifted up as the serpent was lifted up by Moses in the wilderness, so that everyone who has faith in him may in him possess eternal life (3 : 14).

Here union with the Son of Man and the 'only-begotten Son of God' is brought about by faith.   These two aspects are also found in St Paul, and led Deissmann to assert that in St Paul's case, at least, it was not baptism that was decisive, but the appearance of Christ before Damascus.   He held that in every case it was God's grace that alone was decisive.[1] Schweitzer, on the other hand, giving to the Son of Man concept of Daniel the 'corporate' connotation, and seeing in the 'community of the saints of the Most High' the precursor of the Catholic Church, insisted that entrance into

[1] 'The assertion that in St Paul baptism is the means of access to Christ I take to be incorrect.   There are passages which, if taken in isolation, might be held to prove it (i.e. Gal. 3 : 17), but I think it is more correct to say that baptism does not bring about but only sets the seal to the fellowship of Christ.'   (op. cit., pp. 130, 131.)

P.J.M.—H

life 'in Christ' is brought about by baptism alone, and that
for St Paul the relationship of faith in Christ to union with
Christ is that, where faith is present, union takes place
automatically on condition that the believer is baptised.
The entrance into the 'corporeity of the community of
saints' is by baptism.   He saw the peculiarity of St Paul's
mysticism to lie in this very fact, that without baptism there
was no 'being-in-Christ', and that this was therefore not a
subjective experience, but something that *happened* at a
certain moment.   The two aspects found in the Johannine
teaching he considered to be the great enigma of the discourses in that Gospel.

This must probably be regarded as an insoluble question.
It is actually one with which the Church was faced in the
very earliest days, for martyrdom was always held to take
the place of baptism.   Some of the Fathers interpreted the
double stream from the sacred side of Christ as signifying
the two baptisms: that of water and that of blood, that is,
of martyrdom.   'Martyrdom is another baptism, whence
also blood and water flowed from the wound in the Lord's
side.'[1]   If then, martyrdom could take the place of baptism, why not a perfect and living faith?   In the earlier
centuries, too, there was much hesitation in offering one-
self for baptism, because of the gravity of post-baptismal
sin; it was frequently deferred till the death-bed, when
there was no longer any fear of falling into mortal sin.[2]

[1] Tertullian: *De Pudic.* xxii, p. 435.

[2] St Basil, though the son of Christian parents, was not baptised till the
age of 21 or 29.   St Gregory Nazienzus only after attending the schools in
Caesarea, Palestine and Alexandria.   He was caught in November gales on
a voyage to Athens, and for twenty days his life was in danger.   Immediately
on landing he presented himself for baptism.   St Augustine, though his
mother was a Christian, was not baptised till he was 33 years of age.   (See
J. H. Newman: *Essay on the Development of Christian Doctrine*, p. 411.)

When we think of people like Simone Weil, so full of faith and love, so conscious of union with Christ, yet un-baptised, we cannot be too dogmatic on this point. The normal way of the Christian life, of union with Christ, is through the sacraments, but we must remember that God is not bound by the sacraments, and where he finds a soul able to respond to his grace he may confer upon it his choicest gifts quite apart from the sacraments.

Now, though it is true that our life 'in Christ' is normally brought about by the sacraments, the sacraments do not *in themselves* convey mystical experience. They are the 'out-ward and visible sign' of inward grace. Naturally, this does not mean that, at least in the case of the Eucharist, we may not 'taste and see', but only that the grace given in the sacraments is usually hidden from us, though it is not for that reason any less real and effective. What it does mean is that, partaking of them by faith, the full implica-tions of them do often escape us. Since most of us have now been baptised in infancy, and have not known the wonder of coming out of darkness into the light of Christ, this is probably especially true of baptism. The contro-versies of recent centuries have also tended to concentrate our attention on the Eucharist, and thus to turn our thoughts and interest away from baptism, though the balance has probably been restored during the past decade.

The Baptism of Jesus, in spite of its importance in the Gospels and in much of the thought of the early centuries of Christianity, was not brought into direct connection with Christian baptism in the primitive Church. St Ignatius of Antioch sees no connection between the Baptism of Jesus and that of his followers.

> Jesus was born and baptised [he wrote] in order that by his
> passion he might purify the water (*Ad Eph*. 18, ii).

Neither does Justin see any connection between them
(*Dial*. 138).   In fact, not till St Irenaeus (*Adv. Haer*. 3,
ix, iii), at the end of the second century, do we find the
thought that Jesus by his baptism created Christian baptism.
From a very early date, however, both baptism and eucharist
were brought into direct connection with the Passion and
death of Christ.   Jesus himself surely made this connection
in Luke 12 : 50:

> I have a baptism to undergo, and how hampered I am until
> the ordeal is over.

Clearly this must refer to his Passion and Death.   It is on
this thought that we will chiefly dwell.

The origins of Christian baptism are actually somewhat
obscure.   The early accounts in Acts are confused.   At
times the Holy Spirit is given immediately upon believing,
and this is followed by baptism, as at Caesarea when St
Peter had been preaching to Cornelius and his friends the
Holy Spirit came upon all those who listened to the message
he proclaimed.   The Jews who had come with Peter were
amazed that the gift of the Holy Spirit should have been
poured out on these Gentiles, for they heard them speaking
in tongues of ecstasy and praising God.

> Is anyone prepared to withhold water for baptism from these
> persons, who have received the Holy Spirit just as we did
> ourselves? (Acts 10 : 47).

asked St Peter, and ordered them to be baptised 'in the
name of Jesus Christ'.   In other accounts believers had
been baptised 'into the Name of the Lord Jesus', but the
Spirit had not come upon any of them,

So Peter and John laid their hands on them and they received the Holy Spirit (Acts 8 : 17).

In any case we may infer that the Trinitarian formula had not, in the period covered by Acts, come into use, and that it was possible to receive the gift of the Spirit immediately upon believing in Christ, before baptism or the laying-on-of hands by the Apostles. Certain points, however, stand out clearly: that it was essentially the same baptism as that of John the Baptist—unto repentance and remission of sins, in preparation for the Holy Spirit, and that the coming of the Spirit was, certainly at first, thought of in terms of the prophet Joel, in signs and visions. Yet there was this difference: the promised One had come, and they were baptised in the 'name of the Lord Jesus'. Thus baptism became Christocentric, and the way was prepared for St Paul's penetrating insight into the true meaning of Christian baptism.

In the First Epistle to the Corinthians, chapter 10, St Paul speaks of 'baptism into the fellowship of Moses in cloud and sea', and declares that the supernatural food and drink that accompanied the Fathers of the Old Testament in their wanderings was Christ:

> they all ate the same supernatural food; I mean, they all drank from the supernatural rock that accompanied their travels—and that rock was Christ (1 Cor. 10: 3, 4).

He goes on to warn his converts, however, that, great as were their spiritual privileges, it was still possible to forfeit the grace of God, as their forefathers had done in the wilderness. Thus he introduces an ethical element which marks off his sacramental teaching at once from that of the mystery-religions. The most important differences between the religion of the ancient pagan 'Mysteries' and Christianity lay in the fact that the latter was strongly ethical—an element which found no place in the 'Mysteries'—and that the Church is founded upon historical fact, upon the Person of Jesus Christ, whereas the background of the Greek mysteries was mythical, based on the old fertility rites.   One of the main points of resemblance between the two religions was that they were both 'sacramental', and in both mystical union with the Divinity was brought about by sacraments. The very survival of Christianity after the hope of an early return of Jesus was lost may, quite possibly, be attributed to St Paul's teaching that redemption is closely bound up with the *Person* of Jesus and sacramental union with him. Thus Christianity survived in the sacramental life of the Church.   In 1 Corinthians 13 St Paul speaks of the dazzling effects of the gifts of the Holy Spirit which characterised the Apostolic Age, but he is not carried away by them:

> Though I speak with the tongues of men and of angels but
> . . . am without love, I am nothing (1 Cor. 13: 1, 2).

The description of Christian charity which follows shows that the true gift of the Spirit of Christ is not in spectacular gifts but in the inward working of his Spirit, till the whole inner man is transformed into the likeness of Christ.   Both in the Pauline and the Johannine teaching this transformation is brought about by the sacraments.

The Epistle to the Romans contains the heart of St Paul's baptismal teaching:

> We were baptised into union with Christ Jesus . . . into his death (6: 3).

> By baptism we were buried with him (6: 4).

What did St Paul really mean by those words? A death unto sin, and a rising to newness of life? Yes, that certainly, for the Lord our God is holy, and must recoil from sin:

> God's hatred of sin can be propitiated only by the abolition of sin. Christ deals with sin by setting us, at the cost of his Life, in a relationship in which sin can be done away . . . The total work of God's salvation included the incarnation, life, death, resurrection and heavenly session—a single saving act by which the Second Person of the Trinity shared all that is human, sin alone excepted, in order that we might be united with him by baptism and thereby share his life.[1]

God through Christ dealt with sin, and redemption was achieved. In him all Christians are freed from slavery to sin and death, that is, to all the results of the Fall.

The connection of Christ's death with sin is implicit in the New Testament teaching, but St Paul says little about forgiveness. He does not represent it as the object for which Christ died: that *end* was rather justification and reconciliation. The Life of Christ is the manifestation of the grace of God, *not* a means whereby his favour is won. God's will is shown to be a will to redeem; he longs to receive men to himself, yet he cannot deny his own righteousness. The relation of the Cross to sin is a distinctively Pauline conception. In baptism we are brought into the sphere of Christ's saving work, and therefore into union with the Crucified, for it is he himself, in his own Person, who is our salvation. For St Paul the primitive view of baptism was inadequate. He nowhere develops the thought that baptism brings about the forgiveness of sins and the

[1] D. E. H. Whiteley: 'St. Paul's Thought on the Atonement', *J.T.S.*, 1957, p. 240.

possession of the Spirit, because in his view a comprehensive redemption is obtained by baptism, of which forgiveness is but a partial manifestation.   He explains baptism as the basis of the mystical 'being-in-Christ', which goes far beyond anything that primitive Christianity had taught about baptism: his view is much more profound: a true development.

St Paul teaches that in baptism we are brought into union with Christ; it is the true beginning of our life 'in Christ'. The natural symbolism of plunging into the water has, in a sense, become meaningless for him.   Though it is true that the ocean may suggest to us a physical image of the profundity and immensity of God, of his omnipotence and eternity, yet for St Paul the vast 'subconscious' into which we are baptised is no longer the natural element of water, but rather the divine Person of Christ: it has become wholly supernatural.   Baron von Hügel once compared the conscious life to that small portion of an iceberg which appears above the surface of the ocean, while the 'unconscious' might well be represented, he thought, by the vast bulk of the iceberg which is hidden in the depths of the ocean. It is an illuminating comparison.   The 'subconscious' part of the whole human personality, though hidden from our perception, is now known to be of very great importance to the whole of our life; it is one of the great discoveries of recent times.   The immense value of infant baptism lies in the fact that thus the early, formative years of life are lived 'in Christ'.   St John of the Cross insisted that the 'betrothal' on the Cross is made once for all when God gives to the soul the first grace, which comes to each Christian in baptism, while the 'mystical betrothal' is

> after the way of perfection, which takes place only gradually and by stages; and, although both are one, the difference is

that one is wrought at the soul's pace, and so is gradual, while the other is according to God's grace, and thus is wrought once and for all (A. Peers: *Works of St John of the Cross*, Vol. 2, p. 313).

Or, to put it differently, by baptism we are brought into Paradise, into Christ, though only in the mystical life do we attain to a realisation of what this truly implies, and as we enter more and more deeply into union with him we do 'taste and see'; we know that we have come into the Promised Land 'flowing with milk and honey'. The very highest stage of mystical union with God is only the perfect realisation and fulfilment of that life of union which is ours in baptism.

What, however, did St Paul mean by the last words of this verse: 'we are baptised into his death'? There are many possible interpretations. Dr Schweitzer sees it to mean that the effects of baptism are union with Christ in his death and resurrection, which prepares the way for sharing in his glory:

> For St Paul the dying and rising again which begins in baptism annuls all distinctions: Jew and Greek are brought together into one body and together form the new humanity 'en Christo'.[1]

Dr Barrett says:

> In baptism Christians have already put on Christ, entering into him by incorporation into his crucifixion.[2]

This is a point to which we will return later.
Professor Dodd considers that

[1] op. cit., p. 263.
[2] *The Epistle to the Romans*, p. 254.

> The particular aspect of this union with Christ to which Paul here desires to call attention is the sharing of his death. Our old self has been crucified with him . . . Thus the first conclusion we draw is the assurance of our immortality.[1]

Though it is true that St Paul speaks of being 'con-crucified' with Christ, of daily 'dying with Christ', yet this is not the language he uses with regard to baptism. We are baptised not into Christ's 'dying' but into his 'death'—a distinction which it is important to remember. We are 'buried with him' (Col. 2 : 12) in baptism.   Neither does St Paul's language here imply a death to self, though in a sense that is implied.   He says 'ἐις τὸν θάνατον'—'into *his* death'.   Into union with Christ in his death.   May it not mean that in baptism we are 'plunged' into that per-fected Life of the Incarnate Lord which at the *moment* of his death upon the Cross was released and set free to enter into the Life of the Blessed Trinity which was his home (John 3 : 14), taking with him into the Heavenlies, into the Life of God, that perfect humanity which was his? Thus, plunged into his death we are at the same moment plunged into the Life of the Blessed Trinity, submerged, as it were, in love.   At that moment—the moment of Christ's death—the eternal and the temporal interpenetrated, the temporal was taken up into the eternal, and the Holy Spirit of Christ could be outpoured upon the new creation, redeemed humanity.   Thus, quite apart from the dominical command in Matthew 28 : 19 it was perfectly logical to baptise into the name of the Blessed Trinity instead of into 'the name of Jesus', though they mean the same thing, for 'in him was all the fullness of the Godhead bodily', and

[1] *The Epistle to the Romans*, p. 88.

Through him God chose to reconcile the whole universe to himself, making peace through the shedding of his blood upon the cross—to reconcile all things, whether on earth or in heaven, through him alone (Col. 1 : 20).

For Christians a new life has begun which was created by Christ. Father Thornton drew attention to the two aspects of our identification with Christ in St Paul's teaching: in Galatians we become partakers in Christ through our inclusion in him by baptism:

> Baptised into union with him, you have all put on Christ as a garment (3 : 27),

whereas in 2 Corinthians the identification takes place at the moment of Christ's death upon the Cross:

> He died for all, that they which live should not henceforth live unto themselves but unto him which died for them, and rose again (2 Cor. 5 : 15) (A.V.).

> He hath made him to be sin for us, who knew no sin; that we might be made the righteousness of God in him (2 Cor. 5 : 21) (A.V.).

Yet these two 'moments' of identification are not mutually exclusive, and there are indications of both views in the two Epistles. A contrast remains, however, in the Apostle's writings

> between identification associated with the death on Calvary and the identification associated with our entry, as individuals, into the Christian life.[1]

* * *

Though St Paul thus makes baptism personal—'into Christ'—he really does little to help us to understand what

---

[1] L. Thornton: *The Common Life in the Body of Christ*, p. 57.

this implies: he says practically nothing of the earthly life of Christ—that life in which the Heart and Being of God were manifested in this world, in time and space, at least as far as that was possible, for we must never forget that he is the 'incomprehensible' God. For this we must turn to the other New Testament writings.

Hebrews, which was probably written about A.D. 60, assigns much more importance to the Gospel story than does St Paul. The writer does so

> because he believes that Christ's sinlessness and his perfect humanity were essential to his mission.[1]

He 'learned obedience by the things that he suffered', and is thus able to sympathise with us in our weaknesses; for the joy that lay ahead of him Jesus endured the Cross, and we must have our eyes fixed on him from start to finish. He is 'the same yesterday, today and for ever' (13: 8), the 'great shepherd of the sheep' (13: 20). He was in all things tempted like as we are, yet without sin (4: 15). 'In that he himself suffered being tempted, he is able to succour them that are tempted' (2: 18). He learned obedience in the school of suffering, and

> once perfected, became the source of eternal salvation to all who obey him (5: 9).

The writer also gives us the thought that it was necessary for Jesus to 'taste death for every man', since it 'became him, for whom are all things, and through whom are all things, to make the author of their salvation perfect through sufferings, that through death he might bring to nought him that had the power over death, that is, the devil'

[1] C. V. Taylor: *The Person of Christ in New Testament Teaching*, p. 91.

(2 : 9, 14).   It is this Jesus we see crowned with glory and honour.

The First Epistle of St Peter, whether it is in part a baptismal Liturgy for the Paschal Vigil, as suggested by Dr Cross, or not, is in any case of interest in connection with baptism. Though doubts have been cast on its authorship, it has many primitive features, and many scholars now place its date between A.D. 63 and 65, and ascribe it to the Apostle himself, though actually written down by Silvanus (1 Pet. 5 : 12).

In the second chapter there are some points to be noticed in connection with baptism. St Peter, like St John, speaks of 'rebirth':

> Like new-born infants you are, you must crave for pure milk (spiritual milk, I mean), so that you may thrive upon it for your souls' health (2 : 2).

This has led some scholars to see here the influence of the Hellenistic mystery-religions, in many of which the idea of the necessity of rebirth for their votaries was common. This conception, however, as we have already seen, was also perfectly familiar to the Jews of that period in connection with converts to Judaism. In connection with the words 'pure milk' there is ample evidence from the second century onwards that, at least in the Church of Rome, a chalice of milk and honey was administered to the newly baptised, as well as the chalice of wine and water, at their first communion, and it is possible that the custom may have arisen out of this verse. Hippolytus, in the *Apostolic Tradition* xxiii, says:

> At the baptismal eucharist is to be offered, not only bread and wine, but milk and honey mingled together, in fulfil-

ment of the promise to the Fathers, wherein he said, I will
give you a land flowing with milk and honey, which Christ
indeed gave, even his flesh, whereby the faithful are
nourished like little children.

At the end of this same chapter we are given a description of Jesus in terms, it is true, of Isaiah 53 and the
'suffering servant' conception, yet producing the picture
of a real person

in whom was no guile, who when he was reviled, reviled
not again.

Christ suffered on your behalf, and thereby left you an
example; it is for you to follow in his steps (2 : 21).

The meekness and patience of Jesus must have made a very
deep impression on the Apostolic band: it is a note that
rings through all their writings.   In the great 'baptismal'
passage in 1 Peter 3: 18, it meets us again:

Christ also died for our sins once and for all.   He, the just,
suffered for the unjust, to bring us to God.

Then follows the extremely difficult passage, which has
been given a variety of interpretations all down the ages:

In the body he was put to death; in the spirit he was brought
to life.   And in the spirit he went and made proclamation
to the imprisoned spirits.   They had refused obedience long
ago, while God waited patiently in the days of Noah and
the building of the ark, and in the ark a few persons, eight in
all, were brought to safety through the water.   This water
prefigured the water of baptism through which you are now
brought to safety.   Baptism is not the washing away of bodily
pollution, but the appeal made to God by a good conscience;
and it brings salvation through the resurrection of Jesus
Christ, who entered heaven after receiving the submission
of angelic authorities and powers, and is now at the right
hand of God (3 : 19–22).

Christ suffering and Christ triumphant—'Christus patiens' and 'Christus victor'.   He who suffered for us, the great 'Shepherd and bishop of our souls', is also the great Victor on a cosmic scale:

> What Christ exemplified [says Dr. Selwyn] was not only the dying life, in which Christians must strive to follow him, but the dying life triumphant on a cosmic scale—a scale which embraced in its redemptive scope all history back to the Flood, and all reality, unseen as well as seen, beyond this earth as well as on it.   And the crucial point at which this impinges on men's lives is baptism.[1]

The Victor over all the powers of evil is the 'Shepherd and guardian of our souls' (2 : 25), who bore the extremity of pain on our behalf in utter patience and meekness; who, in the words of St Paul 'loved me and gave himself for me' (Gal. 2 : 20).   Into the great stronghold of that triumphant Love we are brought when we are baptised into the 'death of Christ' : into that *timeless moment* when the temporal and the eternal interpenetrated.   Fittingly, this Death was on a cross, for thus it symbolises, as no other sign could do, the interpenetration of time and eternity, of the human and the divine.

Many other questions arise in connection with this whole passage which we cannot deal with here, but there is one point which must be mentioned because of its close bearing on our theme: the mention of Noah and the ark.   In the type-theology of the early Church the parallels were as much between persons as between events and things, so Noah and his company are as much a type of the Christian community as the Flood-water is of the water of baptism. Each time St Cyprian mentions this passage in connection

[1] E. G. Selwyn: *The First Epistle of St Peter*, p. 318.

with baptism he makes the parallel between Noah and the Christian Church (*Ep.* lxxiii, 11; lxxiv, 15; lxxv, 2):

> The one ark of Noah [he says] was a type of the one Church.

Justin, too, says:

> The Church is another race, regenerated by Christ through water and faith and wood, which contained the mystery of the Cross, as Noah, too, was brought safe in wood, floating on the waters with his family (Dial. 38).

There has always been a connection between the wood of the ark and the wood of the Cross of Christ. In the great Passiontide hymn attributed to Bishop Venantius Fortunatus in the sixth century we find the words:

> Bend thy boughs, O Tree of Glory:
>   Thy relaxing sinews bend;
>   . . .
> And the King of heavenly beauty
>   On thy bosom gently tend:
> Thou alone wast counted worthy
>   This world's ransom to uphold;
> For a shipwreck'd race preparing
>   Harbour, like the Ark of old.

As was the case with the Baptism of Jesus, this passage in 1 Peter was not used doctrinally till the second century, when a close association was made between Christ's descent into Hades and baptism. The starting-point of this association of ideas was probably the word '$\dot{\alpha}\beta\nu\sigma\sigma\sigma$', that is, the deep waters of the underworld—the 'tehôm'—which was thought to be the source of all the springs of the earth as well as the sea, and which was held to be the abode of demons and monsters. Early baptismal rites affirmed that the waters were terrified at Christ's coming for baptism, and Origen extended this terror to the powers of the underworld who inhabited these waters. In a sense Christ's baptism involved a Harrowing of Hell. It was therefore not difficult to transfer the idea of the baptism of Christians to the 'Descensus' accompanying the Passion of Christ, for the purpose both of his descent into Hades and of Christian baptism was the release of men's souls from bondage to the powers of evil. Christ's proclamation to the spirits in prison was to let them know that the rule of the evil spirits was over, and that they could no longer dominate the lives of men. In all the main baptismal rites, both in East and West, the renunciation of the devil has a place. This renunciation was always made towards the West. Traditionally, Christ on the Cross inclined his head towards the West, and therefore, says St John Damascene

> We pray towards the east, in order to turn towards him (*De Fide Orthod.* IV, 12, P.G. 94. 1134).

Because of the close connection of baptism with Christ's death and resurrection it took place, from a very early date, during the great Feast of the Pasch, when Good Friday and Easter, death and resurrection, were celebrated together as the one great Feast of the Church.

> Christ, who only is sinless [runs the Easter sequence], reconcileth sinners to the Father. Death and life have contended in that combat stupendous: the prince of life, who died, reigns immortal.

The descent into Hades was part of Christ's triumph over death. To complete his victory over the devil he followed him to his stronghold to snatch his throne—the throne of the 'prince of this world'—and enchain him. In the

P.J.M.—I

West the 'juridical' view of the Atonement has caused this aspect to fall into the background.

*   *   *

In the sub-Apostolic age, after the fading out of the eschatological expectation, there was a tendency for the grandeur of the New Testament theory of baptism to fade away. The second-century writers failed to appreciate St Paul's doctrine, and this led to a certain dimming of the significance of both the sacraments, but especially of baptism.

> The outline of the Early Church's teaching on baptism became blurred and confused as a result of a failure to maintain a hold on the full meaning of the central idea of 'en Christo', for in the conception of being 'in Christ' there is summed up the thought of all the gifts of grace which the justified sinner receives—remission of sins, the status of sonship, assurance of inheritance of the Kingdom of Heaven and of the consummation of the 'adoption' in the redemption of the body, and the indwelling presence of the Holy Ghost.[1]

Thus baptism ceased, in some degree, to have its centre in the saving work of Christ, and the gifts bestowed came to be thought of in isolation from the Atonement, in which they had their origin.

Justin Martyr speaks of regeneration and cleansing from sin, and of baptism as a 'bath of illumination', while Tertullian says it is 'a washing away of our early blindness'. The link between washing and illumination was supplied by John 9, and the name '$\phi\omega\tau\iota\sigma\mu\sigma$' was early applied to the

[1] G. W. H. Lampe: op. cit., p. 150.

rite. The thought is found, too, in Titus: 'The washing and regeneration of the Holy Ghost, which he shed on us abundantly through Jesus Christ our Saviour' (3 : 5 (A.V.)). There was a ready response to such ideas in the thought of the time, for the mystery-cults had their lustrations and their promise of regeneration, and it is therefore no wonder that the Christian apologists were only too ready to grasp the opportunity of describing baptism as the *true* illumination, the true means of rebirth to newness of life.

Very early, too, there was a transition from the custom of baptising 'into the name of Jesus', which is found in the period covered by Acts, to baptism into the 'name of the Father, the Son and the Holy Spirit'. This may possibly have helped to obscure the thought of baptism into the 'death of Christ'. Baptism was thought of under a variety of aspects, many of which are summed up by St Cyril of Jerusalem in the Introductory Address to his Catechetical lectures:

> It is a ransom of captives; the remission of offences; the death of sin; the regeneration of the soul; the garment of light; the holy seal indissoluble; the chariot to heaven; the luxury of paradise; a procuring of the kingdom; the gift of adoption (Cat. Lect. (10)).

It was also frequently compared with fire, and therefore the lesson of the Three Children was appointed for the Easter Vigil:

> A new art the chief artist put forth . . . the womb of the water should conceive . . . As a furnace he recasts bodies in baptism; and as in fire he consumes the weeds of immortality . . . By the heat of the Spirit he purges the rust of body and soul (*Tests and Studies* VIII, Camb. Tr., R. H. Connolly).

The great baptismal controversy between St Cyprian of Carthage and Pope Stephen of Rome at the end of the third century is of interest quite apart from the light it throws on the question of heretical baptism.   Cyprian's view was that only those who had been baptised in the Church had received valid baptism, and that all those who had received heretical or schismatic baptism must be re-baptised into the Church.   Stephen, however, was firm that baptism was once and for all, and that it did not depend upon the priest who had administered it.   Yet he was equally insistent that those who had received baptism outside the Catholic Church must be received into it either by the laying on of hands or confirmation, because only in the Church could the Holy Spirit be received.   As far as we can judge from the writings of Cyprian's party—since the correspondence of the Roman side is not extant—the reason for Pope Stephen's attitude was that baptism had been administered in the name of Jesus Christ (*Cyp. Ep.* 73, 4).   Probably the insistence of Hermas on the importance of the name in baptism had impressed itself on the Church of Rome (which in those early centuries always came out on the right side), an impression so great that any baptism into the 'name of Jesus' was held to be valid.   Incidentally, it was not till the Council of Trent that this was finally forbidden.

Stephen's attitude is interesting because it insists on the absolute character of baptism into union with Christ.   It is ontological, and not merely ecclesiological.   Yet only in the Church—Christ's Body in this world—can the Holy Spirit be received.   It must not be thought from this, however, that confirmation completes Christian initiation, for that is absolutely complete in baptism.   Ie later rite the Holy Spirit is given so that Christ's image may gradually be formed in his children in this present life. The faithful recipient of baptism is united with Christ in his death and resurrection at the moment of baptism, and therefore receives the seal of the Spirit and the image of God. Origen was quite clear, however, that the effect of baptism is neither sudden nor momentary. It is, in a sense, given at a particular moment of time, but it has to be worked out in the power of the Holy Spirit throughout one's earthly life. This conception was strongly developed by Gregory of Nyssa and the Greek Fathers, and is one of Origen's important contributions to the theology of baptism.

The Pauline doctrine of baptism into the death and resurrection of Christ is dwelt upon by many of the later patristic writers, both in East and West, and is much to the fore again by the middle of the fourth century. St Basil dwells on the thought of resurrection in baptism:

> What can be more akin to baptism than this day of Easter? [he asks]. For this day is the day of the Resurrection, and Baptism is a power to resurrection. Dost thou worship him who died for thee? Allow thyself then to be buried with him in baptism, for if thou be not planted in the likeness of his death, how shalt thou be partaker of his resurrection? (Hom. 13 in *S. Bapt.* i, 2, t. ii).

St John Chrysostom insisted that Christ's victory over sin was greater than his victory over death:

> We, having died a double death, arise by a double resurrection; one, at that time from sin, for we were buried with him in baptism. This is the one resurrection, the delivery from sin; the second resurrection is of the body. He hath given the greater; await we the less also; for this is far greater than that; for it is greater to be freed from sins than to see a body raised (*Adv. ebrios. et de resurr.* 4).

This is interesting, for it makes clear the fact that at baptism we are made partakers, then and there, of Christ's resurrection, whereas our own resurrection—that of the body—lies in the future.

In the 'De Sacramentis' which many scholars now attribute to St Ambrose there are references to the Cross in connection with baptism.   In the short interrogative creed it quotes the form:

Dost thou believe in the Lord Jesus Christ *and in His Cross*?

The words in italics are not found in any other baptismal creed or rite.   Again, he says to his neophytes:

What is water without the Cross of Christ?   A common element.   Baptism and the Cross are seen as a single mystery; they cannot be separated.

Etheriea, visiting Palestine towards the end of the fourteenth century, described the customs of the Church at Jerusalem.   During Lent the catechumens were instructed in the Faith, but not till after their baptism at Easter were they initiated into its deeper mysteries.   Day by day in Easter week the gates being closely watched so that none but those who were already baptised should gain admittance, the Bishop spoke to them of the deep things of God.   One of these lectures 'on the Mysteries' in the Catechetical Lectures of St Cyril is on Romans 6: 3, and gives a vivid picture of the baptismal rite of that day, and of the meaning attached to it:

As soon as ye entered into the inner chamber for baptism ye put off your garments . . . having stripped yourselves ye were naked, in this imitating Christ, who hung naked on the Cross, and by his nakedness spoiled principalities

and powers, and openly triumphed over them on the tree
. . . and each of you was asked whether you believed in the
name of the Father and of the Son and of the Holy Ghost,
and ye made the saving confession, and descended three
times into the water, and ascended again . . . In descending ye saw nothing, as in the night, but in ascending again
ye were born as in the day. And at the *self-same moment* ye
died and were born: and that water of salvation was at once
your grave and your mother . . . your birth went hand
in hand with your death . . . Upon Christ death came in
reality . . . but in your case only the likeness of death
and sufferings, whereas of salvation, not the likeness, but the
reality.

10

St John's Sacramental Teaching

BAPTISM IN the Fourth Gospel is that of John the
Baptist: by water in preparation for the Spirit.

Except a man be born of water and the Spirit, he cannot
enter into the kingdom of God (3: 5).

In this Gospel water is frequently mentioned in connection
with the 'signs' of Jesus: at Cana the water is turned into
wine, symbolising the Eucharistic Feast; the Samaritan
woman is told of the 'living water' that Jesus could give;
in place of the institution of the Eucharist at the Last
Supper the Evangelist gives an account of the 'Pedilavium'
(ch. 13), thus probably bringing the two great sacraments
of the Church together. In chapter 4 (v. 2) we are told
that Jesus himself did not baptise, but only his disciples.
St John is consistent in his emphasis on the need of being
born again of 'water and the Spirit', and also in his teaching
that till after the glorification of Jesus 'The Holy Ghost was
not yet' (7: 39), which is the reading in the majority of the
Greek manuscripts. This may be another reason for the
mention of the 'feet-washing' on the last night of the Lord's
earthly life. Though we cannot know with any certainty
what the writer's intention was in describing this scene, it
is possible that here he wished to show Jesus washing the
feet of his disciples with water—that is, giving them his

own baptismal 'washing' in preparation for the outpouring of the Holy Spirit after the Resurrection. On Easter day he came to them, the doors being shut, and breathed on them, saying

> Receive the Holy Spirit! If you forgive any man's sins they stand forgiven; if you pronounce them unforgiven, unforgiven they remain (20: 22, 23).

Water was an old and widespread symbol, with various connotations. In Jewish symbolism water that came down from above denoted Wisdom, or Holy Spirit. Water as a symbol of life is also a very widespread concept and is frequently found in the Old Testament.

The last mention of water in this Gospel is in 19: 34:

> One of the soldiers stabbed his side with a lance, and at once there was a flow of blood and water.

The early Fathers interpreted the meaning of this double stream in different ways. Some saw in it the source of the two great sacraments of the Church, others thought it signified the two baptisms—that of water and that of blood, that is, of martyrdom, which is thought to take the place of baptism. St John Chrysostom interpreted it as applying to the two sacraments:

> Hence the Sacraments take their beginning; in order that when thou drawest near to the awful Cup thou mayest so approach as drinking from the very Side (*Comm. in Thess.* IV: 15).

St Cyril of Alexandria thought

> God so appointed the fact as an image and firstfruits, so to speak, of the Mystic Blessing and Holy Baptism, for Holy Baptism is really of Christ and from Christ; and the power of the Mystic Blessing springs for us out of the Holy Flesh (Hom. lxxxv, in. loc.).

P.J.M.–I*

Tertullian applied the meaning of the twofold stream to the Church:

> Christ so died that from the wound inflicted on his side the Church, the true Mother of the living, might be shaped,

comparing it with the sleep of Adam (Gen. 2: 21), while Rufinus says:

> So because the fountain of sin and death issued from the first woman who was a rib of the first Adam, the fountain of redemption and life is made to issue from the rib of the second Adam (*De An.*, e. xlii, p. 304).

Westcott saw in the two streams a 'sign of life in death' showing Our Lord's true humanity, and in some sense the permanence of his human life, since, in some mysterious way, though dead, he yet lived. He pointed out that by the sign of 'water and blood' we are brought to the ideas which underlie the two sacraments, and the teaching of chapters 3 and 6 of St John is placed at once in connection with the Passion.[1]

Thus we are brought to the great chapter in which St John gives his eucharistic teaching. With characteristic originality and boldness the Fourth Evangelist lifts his eucharistic teaching out of the context of the Last Supper, connects it with the miraculous feeding of the Five Thousand, shows its fulfilment of Old Testament teaching, and reveals the spiritual nature of the Heavenly Food. The

---

[1] 'Though dead the Lord yet lived, and as he hung upon the Cross he was shown openly to be the source of a double cleansing and vivifying power, which followed from his Death and Life. Blood is the symbol of the natural life, and so especially of the life as sacrificed, and Christ by dying provided for the communication of the virtue of his human Life. . . . Water is the symbol of the spiritual life . . . and Christ by dying provided for the outpouring of the Spirit. . . . It is through the Death of Christ, and his New Life by death, that the life of the Spirit and the support of the whole complex fullness of human life is assured to men.'

occasion for this teaching was the incredulous attitude of his Jewish hearers, whose unbelief caused Jesus to develop the true content of his meaning, so that many departed from him because this 'saying' was too hard: 'How can this man give us his flesh to eat?' The chapter opens with the miracle. Jesus, taking the loaves and fishes which were at hand, gave thanks and distributed them to the people as they sat on the ground. Here the Johannine account differs from that of the synoptic gospels, for in those we are told that the bread was given to the disciples to distribute, whereas here it is the Lord himself who feeds the multitude (6: 11):

> Jesus took the loaves, gave thanks, and distributed them to the people as they sat there. He did the same with the fishes, and they had as much as they wanted.

(This point is actually obscured in the A.V.) From the earliest days this Feeding of the Five Thousand has been connected with the Last Supper in the teaching of the Church. St John, by placing his eucharistic teaching in the course of the active Ministry of Jesus rather than on the eve of his Passion may have wished to emphasise the fact that our salvation was accomplished by the whole of the life of the Incarnate Lord, and not only by his Death. Fish is found in many early pictures portraying the eucharistic feast.

The multitudes, who sought Jesus after the miraculous feeding, when he had departed from them, are told that they have only come after him because they had eaten of the loaves and were filled, not because of the work he had wrought in their midst:

> You must work [He tells them] not for the perishable food, but for the food that lasts, the food of eternal life (6: 27).

Here the Old Testament reference is made, as it was by St Paul in 1 Corinthians 10, where he speaks of being baptised 'into the fellowship of Moses in the cloud and in the sea':

> They all ate the same supernatural food, and all drank the same supernatural drink: I mean, they all drank from the supernatural rock that accompanied their travels—and that rock was Christ (10: 3, 4).

The Jews ask Jesus for a sign such as Moses had given to their ancestors in the desert when he gave them the manna —the 'bread from heaven'—and Jesus answers:

> The truth is, not that Moses gave you the bread from heaven, but that my Father gives you the real bread from heaven.

> Sir, give us this bread now and always [comes the eager request].

> I am the bread of life. Whoever comes to me will never be hungry, and whosoever believes on me shall never be thirsty . . . I have come down from heaven not to do mine own will but the will of him that sent me . . . It is my Father's will that everyone that looks upon the Son and puts his faith in him shall possess eternal life; and I will raise him up at the last day (6: 36–40).

Here salvation, union, are granted to faith alone. This is the first of the great 'I am' sayings in this Gospel, and it might only have the force of the others 'I am the way', 'I am the real vine', but later in the chapter Jesus says quite clearly:

> I am the living bread which has come down from heaven: if anyone eats of this bread he shall live for ever. Moreover, the bread which I will give is my own flesh which I will give for the life of the world. Unless you eat the flesh of the Son of Man and drink his blood you can have no life in you (6: 51, 53).

Thus we are brought again to the two aspects that we find in St Paul: union with Christ by faith and union through the sacramental life, for here life 'in Christ' is clearly connected with eating his flesh and drinking his blood in the eucharist. The Incarnation and the Passion are brought together in one verse, and the eschatological note is sounded.

> Whoever eats my flesh and drinks my blood possesses eternal life, and I will raise him up at the last day. My flesh is real food; my blood is real drink. Whoever eats my flesh and drinks my blood dwells continually in me and I dwell in him (53ff.).

Eternal life is shown to be a possibility here and now, as well as hereafter in eternity. Partaking of the heavenly manna we have eternal life, here and now; life 'in Christ' is a foretaste of everlasting life, and the means whereby it is attained. This is an even more emphatic statement of the union that takes place between the believer and Christ in the eucharist than that given by St Paul in Corinthians. Further, St John shows here, as he does in the Last Discourses, that the union of believers with Christ partakes of the same nature as his own union with the Father, and this goes deeper than the teaching of St Paul in this connection:

> As the living Father sent me and I live because of the Father, so he who eats me shall live because of me (6: 57).

Yet after the emphasis on the absolute necessity of eating his flesh and drinking his blood Jesus proclaims that the 'flesh' profits nothing, and it is his 'words' that are 'spirit and life':

> The spirit alone gives life; the flesh is of no avail; the words that I have spoken to you are both spirit and life (6: 63).

Probably what is here meant is that his words and his works are one, and both must be assimilated and received, and it is made clear that the Body he gives us to eat is the glorified, spiritual Body, though this Food is the fruit of the Incarnation, and could not have been given by any other means.

He who gives us his flesh and blood to be our heavenly food, he who said 'I, if I be lifted up from the earth will draw all men unto me', was not only the spiritual rock of which the Israelites drank, but also he who at all times and in all places draws men to himself, since it is for union with him that they were created.

> Lord, to whom shall we go? Your words are words of eternal life. We have faith, and we know that you are the Holy One of God (6: 68).

*   *   *

The mystical theology of St Paul and St John, rooted in the experience of the 'living God', in the 'vision' of Moses, in the ethical mysticism of Isaiah and Jeremiah, in the expectation of the 'Messiah' and the 'Son of Man', went out into a world athirst for God, for union with the divine in mystical experience. The Mediterranean world of that day was characterised by this search for truth and the things of the spirit, with a strong mystical element which stemmed chiefly from Egypt. In Christianity it found its true fulfilment, and brought to the development of the Christian faith its own experience of the divine. It is a mark of the universality and grandeur of the Christian message that the Church was able to receive into herself all that was best in that other, 'pagan' stream which had prepared the way for Christ, and which, together with the

Old Testament and later Hebrew thought and experience, made Christian mysticism the fullest and richest in the world. For despite all the differences between 'historical, eschatological Christianity' and the 'mysticism of infinity', there is in all mysticism an ultimate unity, since Christ is the 'light that lighteneth every man that cometh into the world' (John 1 : 9). Christian mysticism, however, 'overshadows the non-Christian mysticism by its scope, its richness and diversity'.[1] Christianity developed in those early days not by exclusion but by *inclusion* of the best and truest insights in the vision of the ancient world: of those aspirations and longings which had, in their own way, prepared the world for Christ. There is no mystical experience known to other religious traditions that cannot be found in the history of Christian mysticism, though it is true that the *ethical* and moral content of Christianity— so valuable and distinctive—has often tended to obscure the 'mystical' aspect. Nevertheless, it is this mystical element that is the very heart of all religion, if religion is conceived as the inner union of the inmost being of man with God.

Whereas, on the one hand, certain conceptions prevalent in the religious thought of the pagan world may have tended, during the earlier centuries of the Christian era, to obscure the deeper aspects of St Paul's baptismal teaching, there can be little doubt that the rites and ceremonies, as well as the spiritual insights of the 'mysteries' contributed, whether directly or indirectly, to the development and enrichment of eucharistic practice and devotion, bringing out the full content of the Apostolic teaching as the Hebrew tradition alone could probably never have done.

[1] F. Heiler: Eranos Year Book IV: *Spiritual Disciplines*, p. 204.

Bibliography

Augustine, St	*Homilies on St John*
Bouyer, L.	*The Paschal Mystery*
Broomfield, F. W.	*John, Peter and the Fourth Gospel*
Buber, M.	*'I and Thou'*
	'Moses'
Cross, F. L.	*I Peter*
Cyril, St of Jerusalem	*Catechetical Lectures*
Davidson, A. B.	*Theology of the Old Testament*
Deissmann, A.	*St Paul*
Dix, G.	*Jew and Greek*
Dodd, C. H.	*The Interpretation of the Fourth Gospel*
	The Epistle to the Romans
Durrwell, F. X.	*The Resurrection*
Hooke, S. H.	*Alpha and Omega*
Hoskyns, E.	*The Fourth Gospel* (2 vols.)
Lampe, G. W. H.	*The Seal of the Spirit*
Lossky, V.	*The Mystical Theology of the Eastern Church*
Mersch, E.	*The Whole Christ*
Pourrat, P.	*Christian Spirituality* (4 vols.)
Prat, P.	*St Paul* (2 vols.)
Preiss, T.	*Life in Christ*
Pusey, E. B.	*The Doctrine of Holy Baptism*
Robinson, F. Wheeler	*The Cross in the Old Testamnt*
Schweitzer, A.	*The Mysticism of Paul the Apostle*
Selwyn, E. G.	*The First Epistle of St Peter*
Stolz, A.	*Theologie de la Mystique*
Taylor, C. V.	*Names of Jesus*
	The Person of Christ in New Testament Teaching
Westcott, B. P.	*The Gospel of St John*
	The Epistles of St John
Wikenhauser, A.	*Pauline Mysticism*